ASPECTS OF CULTURE

ASPECTS OF

RUTGERS UNIVERSITY PRESS

CULTURE

Harry L. Shapiro

New Brunswick, New Jersey 1956

to Janice

FOREWORD

Brevity, they say, is the soul of wit. But unfortunately, wit cannot always return the compliment.
In these days of brief titles one might happily fore-
go the wit if only clarity could be assured. I am not
altogether certain what the title of this book,
Aspects of Culture, will suggest to the reader. What
I had in mind in writing it was to set forth the way
the modern discovery of culture provides insights
into our daily lives, our current international problems, our history and our civilization itself. The

definition and description of what an anthropologist means by culture might alone have required the space this book occupies. Many anthropologists have felt the need of even more room—as their full-sized volumes indicate. To deal at all adequately with some of the other themes I have touched on would have made similar demands. But my purpose has not been to write a text or an exhaustive treatise about any of them. I have tried merely by various examples to illustrate some of the ideas to which the concept of culture has given birth and to suggest additional applications that might be profitable to pursue. The examples I have chosen are not necessarily the best for the purpose. They are merely those that happened to occur to me. But I think they do make the general point.

I am aware that some of the things I say are controversial. I trust, however, that disagreement with specific interpretations will not undermine my major premises that culture has made us what we are, affects our daily lives and our history and will determine our future.

I hope it will be evident to the reader that I enjoyed writing these lectures for delivery at the College of Puget Sound at Tacoma, Washington. He can at least judge that for himself from whatever evidence the following pages provide. He cannot, however, know without my expressly telling him so how much I enjoyed delivering them. Few audiences could have been more attentive and appreciative. President Thompson, the officers and the faculty of the College of Puget Sound extended a hospitality beyond the call of duty. The Haley family, whose benefaction made the lectures possible, welcomed me with their customary grace. And if I may allow myself a pathetic fallacy, even Mt. Tacoma revealed herself to help make the occasion memorable.

April, 1956   Harry L. Shapiro
New York City

The 1956 Brown and Haley Lectures are the fourth of a series given annually at the College of Puget Sound, Tacoma, Washington, by a scholar distinguished for his work in Social Studies or the Humanities. The purpose of these lectures is to present original analyses of some intellectual problems confronting the present age.

CONTENTS

1 THE DISCOVERY OF CULTURE

As we survey the past we come to recognize that each age in the history of a civilization is distinguished from all others by the characteristic ideas it entertains and by the activities it pursues. Nowhere is this more evident than in the special developments and in the particular styles of the architecture, painting and sculpture that flourish in each epoch. Distinctive as these esthetic expressions are, they are not the only interests that set off one period from another. There are many others, often less obvious because they possess no surviving physical structure that we can see or because they are

abstract and thus escape general notice. Among
these are the ideas and intellectual concepts that
attract the minds of one period more intensely and
significantly than those of another. Our epoch, like
others before it, has its own array of intellectual
preoccupations. One of them is the concept of what
we have come to call culture. In no other age so
much as in our own, and in that only within the
last century, has the recognition of culture loomed
so large or has it so profoundly affected thought.
It is, I think, safe to say that culture is a modern
discovery.

Since I shall be using the term "culture" from
here on, it may be well to identify now what I shall
be talking about. It is perhaps unfortunate that anthropologists have employed for their purposes a
word of such wide and common usage, meaning
variously, "the art and practice of cultivating, till-
age, cultivated land; the act of improving or developing by education; the refining of the moral and
intellectual nature; civilization; refinement in manners and taste; the characteristic attainments of a
people or social order." These uses of the word
have caused confusion because the anthropologist
does not mean specifically the act of cultivating a
field or the sophisticated appreciation of Bach, El

Greco or **Proust** when he speaks of culture, although in his sense the word might include these manifestations. Culture, as I shall use it, has been defined as *learned behavior*. It includes all the patterned, habitual actions and ideas and values we perform, hold or cherish as members of an organized society, community or family.

This is a broad definition and embraces far more than the common meaning of culture. One might reasonably ask, since it seems to take in so much, what it leaves out. For one thing, it does not include the fundamental drives of behavior, as such. For example, hunger has its origins in the physiological demands of our digestive systems, stimulating us to do something about it. It is not, at this level, culture. But the manner in which we eat, the kinds of food we consume, the methods we have devised to obtain the necessary food, are a part of culture. In the same way, our sex instincts or, if you prefer, drives are physiological in origin but their expression is regulated in specific ways that are customary and habitual in human societies, and these forms fall properly within our definition of culture.

What about the apparently erratic forms of behavior, the individual fantasy or idea, or the antisocial tendencies that some or all of us may exhibit or, perhaps wisely, conceal at one time or another? Here the dividing line becomes more difficult to establish. Some of these apparently individual, unlearned and unorganized facets of behavior or mentality may in effect be reactions to cultural facts, so that their very existence may be characteristic of, or unique to, the culture in which they occur and thus be interwoven with it. Would we have feelings of guilt if there were no notions of sin in our culture? Perhaps, but the form and kind of guilt seem to be affected by what a particular culture regards as sin. Would the analysts have an Oedipus complex to deal with if there were not a dominant father in a socially structured family?

Yet, of course, some of our behavior and our feeling is not specific in a cultural sense. Moreover, our ability to exercise some choice within limits gives us a sense of freedom from cultural restrictions.

The curious thing about culture, now that we have become aware of it and discern more and more clearly its pervasiveness in the very fabric of our lives, is how long it has taken men to achieve the objectivity necessary to appreciate it. Perhaps this need not surprise us, for culture by its nature is not an obvious phenomenon until we have learned to recognize it. From infancy, even from birth, we are conditioned to specific patterns of behavior until they become almost automatic. We are punished for infractions and are praised, or at least escape punishment, for conformity. We learn what is expected of us and what to expect of others; what is admirable and what is not. We acquire goals and ideals; we share them and other conditions with our fellows so that we and they know how to behave in the usual situations that arise in our societies, and thus avoid the necessity of making a constant sequence of conscious and serious decisions. Thus the influence of culture becomes habitual and subconscious and makes life easier, just as breathing, walking and other functions of the body are relegated to subconscious controls, freeing the conscious parts of the brain of this burden and releasing it for other activities. All this means that most of us perform our activities in well-accustomed ways that seem as right as rain and as normal as corn in Kansas. Anything else would seem wrong, peculiar or funny. Like the air we breathe, culture is taken for granted and we are hardly aware of it.

But like the air when it becomes suffused with

fog or smog or when it blows hot or cold, culture
too can take on a vividness which we cannot ignore.
When we meet people of another culture behaving
in unaccustomed ways, we sense the reality of the
phenomenon but our reaction is usually to stigma-
tize such behavior as odd or unnatural. This has
not been altogether uncommon at various times in
the past as well as at various places in the present. Even primitive tribes encounter neighboring
groups of differing traditions and learn, sometimes
to their discomfiture, that there exist standards of
behavior different from their own. The Greeks ob-
served these variations and labeled as barbarians
those who failed to conform to their own standards.
Herodotus himself showed a particularly lively interest in what we would today call anthropological
research, for he assiduously noted the strange habits
and customs of the Egyptians and Near Easterners
whom he encountered on his travels. As civilization
has endured with its ups and downs and its succession of epochs, with their characteristic modes of
thought and behavior, history itself has provided
from our own past examples of the same phenomenon.

But awareness of the products of cultural conditioning is not the same thing as the discovery that

they are the results of a process susceptible to analysis and generalization and that their study not only provides us with a means of understanding the behavior of others but also of ourselves. One finds in earlier students little or no appreciation of culture in this sense. Neither a writer like Tacitus, describing the mores of a contemporary primitive tribe, the Germani, nor Herodotus, visiting the centers of ancient civilization, saw in their anthropological data the implication that they were dealing with a process as valid for themselves as for the subjects of their inquiry.

It is not without significance, perhaps, that culture as a determinant of behavior and as a subject for study and analysis should have emerged into our consciousness only in modern times. Never before in history have men of such diverse cultures come into contact with one another. Beginning with the Age of Discovery, ushered in by Portuguese navigators in the fifteenth century, Europeans have spread all over the world. There is now literally no considerable portion of it that has not been visited, explored and described to some extent by these emissaries. Whole continents filled with natives cut off from the rest of mankind for millennia, with civilizations of a grandeur to astonish their discoverers, have been disclosed. Africa, Australia and the Pacific revealed people of a bewildering variety of cultures undreamed of in the centers of Western civilization.

We are accustomed to think of this age of discovery mostly as a time when knowledge of the shape and extent of the earth was rapidly expanding, a matter of continents and oceans, of rivers and mountain ranges—in short, in geographic terms. But it was many other things besides. For four centuries it was an era of unprecedented discovery in every aspect of nature. New knowledge of all kinds poured into Europe, and by its sheer mass and variety enormously stimulated specialized kinds of scholarship and research, merely to deal with it all and to organize it in usable form. Botanists and naturalists, for example, faced with steady floods of new plants and animals, were kept fully occupied classifying and systematizing them. In fact, I suspect that much of the development of these branches of science in the sixteenth and subsequent centuries came from this source.

But the marvelous kaleidoscope of new knowledge was not confined to animals and plants, to rivers and mountains, to lands and seas. An astonishing array of people and cultures that no one in Europe even knew existed was also discovered. Their number was prodigious and their variety bewildering. Murdock has estimated that something like 3000 distinct cultures can be enumerated. Even if we halve this number to allow for the enthusiasm and the meticulous classification of the anthropologist, we would arrive at an average rate of some three to four new cultures discovered annually over a period of four centuries. It would be hard in the face of this long-continued process of discovery to preserve an insensitivity to cultural variation.

Actually, to the strange systems of behavior encountered, the first reactions seem rather odd. The Spaniards, for example, hardly crediting that human beings would act as they found Indians doing, maintained a rather lively controversy, joined in both by the representatives of the Church and the reporters of the Conquest, on the existence of a soul in the newly discovered inhabitants of the New World. Apparently, some of the Spaniards were not altogether sure whether the creatures they found in America were men or not and whether they were, therefore, proper subjects for conversion to Christianity.

As discovery continued, however, the impact of

such an assemblage of distinctive populations with
apparently bizarre ways of life demanded of European intelligence some frame of reference—an explanation of this astonishing variety of people and
the plethora of customs and manners. Some of the
explanations were, of course, colored by the intellectual milieu of the times. One of them, still with
us, is that of the derivation of the Indians from
the Ten Lost Tribes of Israel. Ten tribes of Israel
were known to have failed to return from the Cap-
tivity; here were people in the New World unac-
countable by descent from the known nations of
the Old World; therefore they must be the descend-
ants of the Lost Tribes. Unfortunately since this
neat solution was used up for the Indians, there
was no room in the scheme for Australian aborig-
ines and the various other natives subsequently
encountered. Moreover there were no other lost
tribes to be accounted for. By this time, anyway,
interest was waning in this easy equation.

But European scholarship continued to seek a
system of classification for these new types and
forms of mankind. At first the effort was made to
fit the newly discovered populations into a classification modeled on the systems set up by naturalists.
Bernier in 1684 was one of the first to attempt such

a systematic classification without, however, any theory as to the origin and dispersal of mankind and with little or no emphasis on culture. Most scholars seemed to find a satisfactory answer for this problem in the Bible, which had the races of man by descent from the sons of Noah, who gradually differentiated from one another in a manner never clarified. We still preserve a vestige of this explanation of racial genesis in our use of "Hamite" and "Semite."

It is probable that European scholars struggled first with the problem of physical diversity in man because they already had established a pattern of thinking about anatomical and morphological differences in their zoological and botanical systems. The physical evidence of variety in man fitted this pre-existing orientation. But a growing awareness of cultural diversity and its meaning soon began to emerge. One begins to encounter at first tentative essays dealing with cultural phenomena and various experiments in handling such data to support migration hypotheses and to establish relationships. By the beginning of the nineteenth century, however, anthropology as a science devoted to the systematic study of organic and cultural man was taking shape, winning the attention of scholars throughout Europe and receiving support from centers of learning.

CULTURE AND COLONIALISM

Although I have suggested that culture as an abstract concept was born of the extraordinary experience of Europeans encountering a new world of customs and behavior in a relatively short period of time, I am not advancing the notion that it would not have developed under other circumstances. The Age of Discovery was a kind of hothouse that may be said to have anticipated the season by bringing to bloom fruits of knowledge that might otherwise have been slower in maturing. But one cannot overlook another significant factor in shaping interest in this problem. From the very beginning of European contact with native peoples, the association was an exploiting one. The Portuguese navigators and Columbus were seeking routes of trade which they hoped to establish for their commercial enjoyment and profit. But whether they succeeded as did the Portuguese, or failed as did Columbus, they all encountered native peoples whom they undertook to exploit for trade or for labor. But these were people living by customs and obeying rules that had to be understood if their conquerors were to succeed in their purposes. One finds, it is true, little evidence that these early explorers, conquerors or entrepreneurs tried very hard to acquire this knowledge, although some accounts of native life even at this date show a sincere if fumbling effort to understand the bases of native custom. But it is all too common to find that the initial European contacts were unhappily characterized by a cultural ignorance that had devastating effects on native populations. Even if some of this decimation can be blamed on disease, epidemics and alcohol, in most cases it was caused by the failure to realize that the culture of a people supports its well-being and that its apparently brutal destruction can be fatal to native populations.

Sometimes colonization turned out to be feasible in those areas where native populations had been destroyed; then the necessity of dealing with native cultures, of course, no longer existed. But where colonization was attempted in areas occupied by aboriginal people, as in Peru, Mexico, South Africa, New Zealand or Kenya, or where a colonial pattern of European control over native people developed, as in India, Malaya, Java and the Philippines the problem of native culture became a leading consideration. It is perhaps not without meaning that native culture under these conditions generally survived where it had attained a high level of technology, usually in the form of agriculture, and supported a fairly dense population. The groups that readily succumbed, with a few exceptions, were the more primitive hunting and gathering people, occupying their areas thinly as their economy allowed. This does not mean that some hunting and gathering peoples have not endured to the present, but they are generally like the Eskimo or the natives of the more remote valleys of New Guinea, surviving because they inhabit regions unfavorable to European encroachment or difficult of access. We can draw from this knowledge the generalization that the survival of a culture when exposed to the hazards of exploitation depends on its level of technical development and the density of its population. And a case might be made for density alone being the critical factor, for when density has been possible without agriculture it seems to provide a safety in itself.

It is this factor that accounts for the broad differences between the colonialism of the New World and of the Old. In general, the colonial areas of

Asia and Africa were never settled and colonized by Europeans, for the simple reason that these areas were already densely populated. The natives did not succumb to European contact and thus never provided the unoccupied space necessary for schemes of settlement. Consequently, we see no important enclaves of Europeans in India, Southeast Asia or the rich and populous adjacent islands. In the New World, however, much of the land was occupied by hunting and gathering groups, thinly distributed. Their economy could not be maintained in the face of European occupation, which had the effect of destroying the very basis of their livelihood. Thus they melted away or, if they attempted to defend their way of life, were easily destroyed since they were too few in number and too poor in arms.

The exceptions, both in the Old World and the New, to this distinction merely serve to prove the general rule. In Peru, Mexico and the Southwest United States where native cultures did survive, they did so because they were based on agriculture, which could be carried on regardless of what happened outside the arable fields. Moreover, agriculture supports denser populations. On the contrary such colonization as took place in Africa, Australia or New Zealand succeeded because it was attempted where native population was thin.

Colonialism had thus brought Europeans into increasingly intimate contact with the peoples of the world. They were, by the nineteenth century, governing enormous areas dominated by cultures previously unknown to them. It soon became apparent that if the task of governing these populations and of directing their labor into profitable channels were to succeed, it was necessary to understand why these people behaved the way they did. In short, European administrators found themselves face to face with culture. The problem was an eminently practical one. The record shows all too frequently a fumbling approach and sometimes a downright obtuseness in recognizing the facts. Some of the early failures must undoubtedly be laid to the misguided efforts of culture-bound Europeans who could conceive of departures from their own cultural values only as deplorable. Their remedy was to treat these manifestations as childish, ridiculous or plain vicious and to attempt to substitute their own culture as soon as possible, by force if necessary. What these proconsuls failed to grasp was that behavior is so delicately interwoven and adapted to a cultural pattern, that roughshod interference with it could either destroy the people themselves or lead to resistance in ways that could not be anticipated, and which could defeat the purposes of their governors.

This colonial experience must have contributed greatly to an awareness of culture, whether the experience were a success or a failure. As this experience has deepened, it has sharpened the interest of scholarship in the same phenomenon. It is not without interest that what seemed like purely academic research by anthropologists with little or no practical value is now proving of the greatest importance in colonial affairs. For the success of colonialism, this recognition has come a little late.

The role of culture, however, is not diminishing as colonialism contracts. It is with us now and will probably continue to be. Consider such programs as Point Four. Here is a scheme to bring the benefits of modern technology to underdeveloped areas. It is a complex idea compounded of truly altruistic aims and practical policy for stabilizing world affairs. To execute the designs of the program, however, processes and values developed in and adapted to one culture must be transferred to quite another. To attempt this without taking account of the cultural situation has often led to difficulties that Point Four administrators quickly realized might wreck the program itself. In fact, one of the major problems turns out to be not the availability of "know-how" or machines or money, but cultural acceptance. It apparently does not occur to us that what is desirable to us is so because it is a part of a training and a nurture we cannot avoid and can scarcely sense. To others, nurtured differently, it may not seem desirable, and to convince them that it is, requires a painful and conscious effort.

Far more serious for the future is the continuing difficulty of cultural understanding in a world of sensitive nationalism, struggle for power and memories of colonialism. To move successfully in such a world, where powerful forces are not averse to using for their own purposes cultural antagonisms and misunderstandings, we must have the basic comprehension of the enormous force which culture represents and the good sense to respond to its subtleties. I venture to predict that in the context of world relationships it will play an increasing rather than a diminishing role, and that we will become more and more familiar with the concepts that it represents. This is an age of culture consciousness.

CULTURE AS ENVIRONMENT

Anthropologists used to be interested in the question of universals in culture—those patterns of behavior that occur in all cultures and which might be regarded as essential or inevitable features. Language, which is an element of culture, is one of them and some form of family organization is another. It would, for example, be hard to see how any culture could maintain itself without language as a means of communication and learning; and no culture could long survive without the protection of the child. But more significant in some ways is the fact that culture itself is universal. There are no aggregations of human beings living together as a population who do not share a culture. In fact, a group of human beings without culture is virtually an impossibility, or at least difficult to conceive. And even the hermit or solitary who thinks he is abandoning the ways of men takes with him unwittingly some of them, for whether he likes it or not his attitudes and ideas, deeply ingrained during his infancy and childhood, are like invisible burrs that stick to him throughout his life.

It is remotely possible that some of the children reported to have been abandoned in the forests in times of stress or famine might survive in a culture-less condition. This practice was said to have been

known in Europe during medieval times and even as late as the eighteenth century. The fairy tale of Hansel and Gretel is thought to be a more palatable transformation of the unhappy custom. Linnaeus might have had in mind just such rare cases when he reserved in his classification of mankind a place for *homo ferus*—or wild man. Recently, reports from India, somewhat controversial in their reliability, described similar instances with circumstantial detail. But even if an occasional child survived such an experience, which seems doubtful on the face of it, any group of them would set about creating a culture since it is in the nature of man to evolve patterns of living.

This universality of culture can very well be explained as a product of human evolution. For man has been able to create culture only because he has evolved the organic and neurological mechanisms that made it possible; but, in thus creating it, man brought into existence another dimension of his environment to which he has had to adapt himself. This is a process that can be understood by first taking a look at the long course of vertebrate evolution leading up to man. The inevitability of culture thus becomes apparent and its effect on human development can be seen as a unique continuation of evolution itself. In the long and complex course of evolution, we find that the multifarious arrangements and patterns of organic life may be explained as adaptations to the almost infinite variety of the environment. The ability of fish to live in fresh or salt water depends upon nephritic and other mechanisms which they develop and which permit them to adjust their physiological functions to the concentration of salt or the lack of it. Fishes, we know, will die when removed from water, yet some of them in the distant past possessed organs they could use to obtain the necessary oxygen from the air instead of from water, and thus manage to live at least for limited periods on land. This adaptation had fateful consequences, for it opened to vertebrates, or creatures with backbones, the opportunity of exploiting for the first time the lands of the world. To make use of the resources of the land such a creature must have some means of locomotion suitable for a relatively solid environment, and the fishy equipment of the first landed vertebrates was quite an inadequate one. Then began the long, slow process of the transformation of an elongated, sinuous body equipped with fins into a four-legged one able to support its own weight and to move with some celerity. It was a process that could abandon the older model only gradually as the new was taking shape. Thus the vestiges of their former condition can be seen in the earliest four-legged vertebrates.

But the land is far from being a simple homogeneous environment. It has hills and dales, plains and mountains, swamps and deserts. It is hot and cold. It has a variety of plants that differ in one place from another. To all these variations of environment, and to many others, the land-living vertebrates adapted themselves by thousands of varying mechanisms by which they were able to get along better in the special conditions that were available. Some environments remained empty to these creatures, for they had not yet evolved the special adaptations that would enable them to enter them. Thus the air, surrounding and blanketing the land, was available to insects, for example, but was closed to the vertebrates until some of them in the reptile stage of their evolution acquired, through some variation, an ability to glide or fly. It is not altogether clear what advantage this new ability gave its possessors. Possibly they could evade pursuers by taking off in this bizarre and novel fashion, and, by thus perfecting their equipment for escape, gained enough survival value out of it so that their kind could flourish. The fossil evidence, however, is clear that once this device became established it was never lost. On the contrary, we see a whole series of improvements on the original model which eventually led to the marvels of bird flight and the entry into still another environment.

The reptiles as a whole display an astounding variety of forms, now mostly extinct, which represented experiments in adaptation to a widening range of environmental niches. Although many of these were directly responsive to the physical environment in which their possessors habitually lived, others seem to reflect adaptation to what one might call the ecological environment, or the world of other creatures disputing the same niche or territory.

The mammals, small and relatively weak at first, eventually gained supremacy over the reptiles by virtue of several highly significant adaptations. Among these was the series of physiological mechanisms that endowed them with more independence of the fluctuations of the temperature around them than their predecessors had. Their ability to regulate their own body temperature and keep it at a specific level, whether the sun shone or not, or whether it was winter or summer, was an enormous advantage. Now, unlike the reptiles, the mammals could range over a greater climatic area and could face virtually all weather. Moreover, modification in the mammalian heart and circulatory system enabled the mammals to dispose of fatigue products more effectively and to supply their bodies more efficiently with oxygen and food. These physiological improvements permitted them to continue high levels of activity over longer periods of time, which in combat, in the hunt, in flight and in various other crises, provided a distinct advantage for survival.

Whether or not the abandonment of egg laying and the bearing of their young within the body had any special survival value is difficult to say. All we can be certain of is that the mammals, after some experiments along this line, eventually became committed to a viviparous form of reproduction, giving birth to helpless young that require varying periods of additional growth and development before reaching sufficient maturity to fend for themselves. It is possible that in some way this method of reproduction is a by-product of other changes. Although as a reproductive device it emphasizes safety rather than numbers, it also opens the possibility of a greatly extended period of development. The hatching of young from eggs sets a limitation of time and place that is eliminated by uterine development. If an egg has to be incubated by body heat, then a protracted incubation period obviously becomes a serious difficulty. On the other hand, if the incubation is left to the heat of the sun, the egg must be abandoned by the mother and left to take its chances. If the incubation period were long, it would limit egg laying to geographic areas where the weather is reliable for extended periods of time. Moreover, the longer an egg is left to itself the greater the hazards to its escaping damage from diverse sources. Thus the mammalian mechanism of the placenta and uterus allows a greatly extended time span for the elaboration of an increasingly complex type of organization. As mammals have evolved, the period of infancy has also been extended in time, allowing for the growing burden of unfinished business. All this has meant that the restrictions of time for developmental purposes have been appreciably lifted and mammals need be less hampered in their acquisition of complex mechanisms.

Another feature, again unforeseen in its potentialities, is the concomitant development of maternal solicitude. Offspring born in a helpless or nearly helpless condition require unselfish care and devotion from the mother. It is a general rule that maternal solicitude develops in direct proportion to the inability of the newborn to take care of itself. The female fish having prepared or selected a proper place for her purposes, lays her eggs and then does little more to ensure their safety. The newly hatched fish born with an ability to swim and find its own food receives no help from mother. The hen in the yard, or the bird in the tree, gives several weeks to hatching her young, who are born in need of some protection and assistance, and for some weeks or months remains a devoted mother. But the period of helplessness is brief and the solicitude lasts only as long as necessary. The mammals, however, display protracted periods of maternal concern continuing in many of them for several years where the infancy of their young is of equal duration. Maternity and length of dependency reach their maximum development in the mammals. I have dwelt on this theme at some length because it is important in culture and I shall return to it later.

From the middle of the Mesozoic (some 150 millions of years ago) when the mammals first appeared, they began to display, as did the reptiles before them, an amazing variety of adaptations to all sorts of environments that their new abilities opened to them. Eventually some became fleet runners with limbs neatly and efficiently developed to the purpose in a variety of ways; others evolved as animals adapted for eating flesh and for preying on other animals. Some became forest dwellers; others took to cold climates. Mammals went underground like moles, and mammals took to the air like bats. Some even returned to watery environments but, unable to recover the ancestral device of the gill, evolved modifications of their air-breathing systems that enabled them to cope with a watery medium.

One group of mammals appearing distinctly only in the Eocene at the beginning of the Tertiary (about 70 to 75 million years ago) took a tack that also led them away from purely terrestrial adaptation. They took to living in trees and became primates. What distinguished these arboreal mammals from others such as squirrels was the fact that they adopted this mode of living early in their mammalian development and before they had modified their ancestral limb and digital pattern very much. A mammal committed to running about on the ground generally evolves in the digital structure of its foot or hand some degree of stability for weight bearing. This is accomplished at some expense to the flexibility of the member as a whole. In extreme cases, as in the horse, the adaptive advantage of stability ends by sacrificing all flexibility, and the terminal segment of the limbs becomes a hoof which through its transformation now permanently limits such an animal to terrestrial life. But some mammals that had only gone part of the way in sacrificing flexibility still found tree climbing a possibility. They took up this mode of life, and they could climb by using their claws as a kind of hook by which to draw themselves up a tree. Their partial adaptation to terrestrial life lost for them the possibility of using their hands or feet as true grasping organs. The timing in the case of the primates was quite different. The ancestors of this order of mammals adopted an arboreal existence at an early stage of mammalian differentiation while they still retained the flexibility of the primitive mammalian hand. To steady the body on a precarious perch in the trees or to move it along a narrow branch, this flexibility and independence of the digits could best be used by grasping with thumb and fingers. This apparently simple, but in fact quite unusual, ability can scarcely be overemphasized. It led eventually to a semi-erect type of locomotion that made fully erect posture possible and it enabled the primates to acquire the ability to grasp an object with one hand and use it as a tool.

Living in trees had another profound influence on the primate precursors of man. To leap from branch to branch placed a premium on a high order of visual acuity and an ability to judge distance, if disaster were to be avoided. As a result, the primates evolved stereoscopic vision by a migration of the orbits to a frontal position in the face, and some of them even acquired color vision. These developments, combined with a grasping hand that could pick up and explore all kinds of objects, are obviously adaptive features of distinct value to tree-living primates. They could scarcely have evolved, however, without concomitant changes in the brain and the elaboration of cortical areas. These three developments, an expanding brain, a grasping hand and an ability to stand fully erect, represent a combination found only among primates and they are what made human evolution possible.

When man's ancestors abandoned arboreal life, these developed primate qualities enabled them to exploit terrestrial life in a way and with a success that their first primate ancestors could not have achieved. But in doing so our ancestors also abandoned using their arms for locomotion as all their primate relatives did and still do. Their ability to take these first upright steps arose from the adaptation to semi-erect posture they had acquired through millions of years in the trees, where using their arms for locomotion necessarily brought their bodies into a vertical position. Moving about on the ground with arms now free of their responsibility for locomotion, these ancestors of ours could put them to other purposes which their relatively well-developed brains could devise.

Up to this point, primate and human progress can be quite adequately explained in terms of adaptation to physical conditions found already existing in nature—a process of fitting specific environmental niches. From here on, however, we can only account for the emergence of man as an adaptation to the culture he has himself created. It is uncertain when he began this unique experiment since the only evidence there is, or indeed can be, is what has survived for us to find. Naturally only material objects could survive and these we can recognize only if they exhibit unmistakable signs of purposeful use or deliberate modification for such use. The earliest recognizable traces are the stone tools, appropriately crude, found in strata one-half million or so years old; when they were made man had already been in existence for some time.

I am not, however, here concerned with tracing the archaeological record of culture, fascinating as that is. I am rather trying to emphasize that the appearance of culture became possible only when man began to use and to make tools deliberately. He could do this only because of his hand, which had been perfected in and inherited from tree-living primate ancestors, liberated from locomotory functions by upright posture, and controlled by a brain endowed with qualities developed by a long arboreal schooling. Many primates show a tendency to use tools and to use them quite ingeniously. The chimpanzees, so amenable to the psychological laboratory, have displayed in a wide variety of situations, set up to test this skill, an ability to size up a problem and to utilize whatever is handy in the way of boxes and sticks to solve it. They can do this more readily than other animals because their hands are fitted for such purposes. But no animal, not even the accomplished chimpanzee, makes tools except man.

It is this tool-making and tool-using skill that lies at the base of culture. Upon it our whole technology has been erected and even our proudest achievements must at last be traced to this fundamental ability which began in so fumbling a manner so long ago. To use the hands in this way sets up a cultural milieu that exercises a selective function of incalculable significance for the development of the brain. And the brain as it develops in turn permits the hands to execute more and more complex manipulations. And so a kind of feedback system is established between hand and brain, mediated by culture as a product of both.

But culture without language is equally inconceivable. Technology is only a part of a culture. And the more complex a culture becomes, the greater the need for communication. Even thought itself, as Sapir has said, depends on language. And thus the power to symbolize and to abstract, which language demands, also exerts a powerful effect on the human brain. In the nascent culture we have been reconstructing, the individual unable to use his hands effectively for tool making and using, and also unable to communicate by language, would be at a serious disadvantage. On the contrary, a skill with tools and a facility in language would favor their possessor. Culture thus becomes an environmental niche into which mankind fits itself. And as culture evolves and becomes more complex and efficient in gaining advantages for those who live by it, it exercises its selection more stringently, eliminating more and more as time goes on those who cannot change with it but remain at the primitive level from which mankind began. It is no wonder, then, after perhaps a million years of a process like this, that man and culture have become inseparable. For man has been adapted over this long stretch of time to a way of life he cannot do without.

The tempo of the evolutionary transformation of an ape-like creature into *Homo sapiens* is in the long retrospect of life itself startlingly rapid. The present estimates allow no more than a million years, which is a tiny fraction of the length of time organic life has existed on this planet. But on closer examination, the transformation is impressive only in the skull and particularly in the size of the brain. Elsewhere in the body the distinctions that exist are far less striking. The brain has expanded enormously during human evolution and is now three or four times the size of that of the largest anthropoid apes, which is probably roughly comparable with that of our earliest man-like ancestors. Since the brain is the seat of intelligence, and intelligence is in a sense an adaptation to culture, as well as an agent of culture, it should not surprise us that it is in this organ that human evolution has been largely centered.

I discussed earlier the increased importance in mammals generally of the prolonged dependence of offspring on maternal solicitude. This tendency is especially evident in the primates, and nowhere more than in the large anthropoid apes and in man. To some extent, of course, the larger the animal, the longer its postnatal development and the more delayed its sexual maturity. The mouse is sexually mature at 39 to 52 days, according to species, the rabbit at 5.3 to 8.5 months, the fox at about one year, the heifer at about a year to a year and one half, and the elephant at 10 to 13 years. But size alone does not adequately account for the slow rate of development in the anthropoids and man. Yerkes says that the female chimpanzee becomes sexually mature at around eight years of age and she is much smaller than a 400 or 1000 pound heifer that matures in a quarter of the time. The human female, but little larger than a chimpanzee, matures at 13 years or thereabouts, on the average. Moreover, in human society the dependence of the child is still further prolonged. This biological phenomenon of delayed maturity in the apes and men is probably associated with the greater role played by the central nervous system in these creatures, and with the longer span of time required for its development and maturation.

But whatever its origin, it provides a significant opportunity for social conditioning and learning, without which it is hard to imagine culture flourishing. Indeed, our own experience is all too impressive on this score. The burden of learning has become so great, as our culture becomes more and more complex, that our children, to acquire the knowledge and education they need, are required to prolong their period of dependency on their parents far beyond the span of their physical and psychological immaturity.

We have reached the point where few medical students, for example, have completed their education and are accepted as responsible practitioners of their skills before the age of twenty-six or twenty-seven—an age which in a simpler society might represent a peak in a social or cultural career, not a mere beginning. We tend to think of young men in their twenties as still unready for full responsibility, when only three or four hundred years ago the great achievements in the time of Elizabeth were accomplished by men as young as this or younger. And in the earlier days of this republic, it was not unusual to find captains of ships and leaders of hazardous expeditions scarcely out of their teens. It may be that the shorter span of life in those days had something to do with providing more opportunity for the young, but regardless of the changing age structure of society, our requirements in general demand longer periods of education than was the case in former times.

If I have stressed the linkages between increasing cultural complexity and the lengthening periods of dependence and learning, I am not unaware of the problem which this creates in our culture. Is it this very dislocation that lies at the root of the current upsurge in juvenile delinquency? At present, boys and girls already stirred by adult emotions, and physically and psychologically ready for at least some degree of responsibility and for a serious place in society, are still confined to a position that allows them little scope for their emergent capabilities. In primitive societies, adolescents play an integral part in the life of the community, with duties and responsibilities that are respected and often vital. Juvenile delinquency as we know it is no problem there; in fact, it does not exist. I am not suggesting, of course, that juvenile delinquency in a society like ours can be explained on this basis alone. It is a complex social phenomenon and has other facets, but the disparity I have described seems to me, on cultural grounds, to be an important one among them.

CULTURE IN A CHANGING WORLD

I have been trying to give some concept of the nature of culture by sketching out some of its dimensions and tracing a few of its ramifications. In doing so, I have selected examples of the way it affects our lives as well as the way it has affected the very beings we have become. Until our own times, culture has, by its very nature, been like the Gulf Stream, flowing steadily, influencing the existence and nature of life wherever its effects were felt, and yet invisible to the untutored eye. Like the sea plants carried in its currents, or the fishes more actively seeking to keep within its milder temperatures to which they had become adapted, man has always subconsciously sought to remain within the limits of his culture and to fit himself to its requirements and demands. This he has done without effort or self-consciousness. It has been a natural process.

The discovery of culture, the awareness that it shapes and molds our behavior, our values and even our ideas, the recognition that it contains some element of the arbitrary, can be a startling or an illuminating experience. It can also be a dangerous one. But above all this emergence of culture, like the pattern taking shape on an exposed film in developing fluid, moves it from the hidden and the unconscious to the visible and conscious.

Culture consciousness had one consequence that might have been foreseen and that still lingers with us. The nature of culture was beginning to be defined at a time when classical colonialism was expanding most actively, and the theory of evolution was being formulated. Culture therefore was regarded both as subject to a development like organic evolution, and as an expression correlated in some way with intellectual endowments and personalities. Although these two ideas are not necessarily dependent on each other, they did become entwined. And in plain language, it became a common belief that the culture any people possessed reflected more or less accurately their capabilities, and thus both cultures and people could be arranged in an ascending order from most primitive to most evolved. It was not difficult under the circumstances for Europeans intent on justifying colonialism to use this assumption. It has been a long and arduous task, apparently not yet fully successful, to demonstrate that neither groups of people nor their customs can be quite so neatly strung on an evolutionary thread. History is full of examples of the lowly in culture inheriting the earth, of the barbarians of one period becoming the highly civilized of the next. The Greeks, the Romans, the French, Germans and British each represented at one stage the uncivilized to their predecessors. Culture development we now know depends on a number of factors, some of them beyond the control of the individuals in a culture, and we are not prepared to assess a people by the culture they happen to have at the present. Culture changes, even though, according to the French aphorism, the more it changes, the more it is the same thing.

But change, by speeding up its tempo, transforms

itself from a process to an active agent capable of the disruption of culture itself. Culture in its initial stages developed so slowly it seems in retrospect almost static. The Paleolithic lasted for hundreds of thousands of years and even its various subdivisions were longer than our entire historic period. With the introduction of agriculture and domesticated animals in the Neolithic, we sense a distinct quickening of the tempo of culture change. The speed picked up still more in the Bronze and Iron Ages. And at present we now experience within generations a rapidity of cultural change that is greater than at any time in the past. Washington and Jefferson would have been more at home in Ancient Rome than in the world of today. We have only to read the novels of Jane Austen, Trollope and Dickens to realize how great is the gulf in technology, manners, class structure and ideals between their day and ours. In the last generation or two, the effect of the automobile alone on our way of life is prodigious. The shape of our cities has been profoundly altered by it. Our individual mobility and ease of communication have enormously expanded. Areas once remote and isolated have been opened up. The country has been covered by billions of dollars' worth of highways.

A vast industry has been created, affecting our entire economy and causing massive population resettlement. It has added a hazard to life equivalent to that of warfare. And it has contributed to a new pattern of behavior in our young and among our not so young. These are only a few of the changes wrought by one technological invention, but they illustrate the speed characteristic of culture change in our time, with the immediate prospect ahead of an even greater acceleration.

All this is in the nature of the development of culture, which grows and evolves by accumulation. Each discovery or invention is added to the sum total of the cultural deposit and opens the way for still newer discoveries. These in turn both widen the areas of exploration and stimulate the rapidity of the accumulation of new advances.

Such a tempo demands, as we have seen, an almost vertiginous modification in culture to keep pace with it. And it has created a dangerous gap between our technological power and our cultural controls. The inherent potentiality of an atomic civilization already terrifies many thoughtful people who find it impossible to place their trust in mankind's wisdom and restraint to manage it without disaster for the people of the earth and perhaps all of our present civilization. Here is the great challenge that faces all of us. It is the gulf between power and wisdom. It has always existed, but in the past the power was less devastating and the wisdom more commensurate with its control. In the past, culture had more time to adjust itself to the dangers, and thus to control or minimize them. And in the past the failure to meet the challenge was local and eventually reparable. Now the gulf is wider than before, and failure would be world-wide and recovery from it problematical. The fears that such a situation evokes express themselves in a variety of ways. A few years ago there was a call for a moratorium on all scientific advances, on the plea that we required time to digest what we had already achieved and created. Many people are now disturbed by what they regard with some real justification as a growing wave of anti-intellectualism throughout the country. Is this a reaction against the uncertainty and tensions created by this gulf, and for which science is held responsible? Is it a kind of fatigue generated by the rapidity of change?

The solution to this paramount problem can be found only through an understanding of culture. We cannot hope to see any profund change in the nature of man through organic evolution. Evolution of that kind is slow. But the nature of man is amazingly flexible and capable of extraordinary adjustments to cultural demands and conditions. We have come to realize not only the profound influence that culture exerts upon us but to appreciate that it is after all subject to change and modification. Whereas in simpler societies these changes are generally accidental, haphazard or unplanned, the need for some degree of conscious control becomes more pressing as society grows more complex. Already with our systems of taxation, social security, agricultural programs and other devices, we are profoundly altering our lives. The answer is not necessarily less control, but a fuller recognition that culture is a whole way of life, and that to modify one of its parts may have unanticipated effects on the whole.

2 CULTURE AND HISTORY

More often than we realize, we are the victims of words. We do not usually think about this, simply because most of the time we talk to other people who share with us a common language and a common culture. The two are so interwoven that our speech provides us with the means of getting along adequately in our own culture. For example, the word "home" represents to us a value and a concept that is so integral a part of the way we live that its absence would be unthinkable. If we had no such word, one would most certainly have to be invented. The word can arouse our deepest emotions and, indeed, thousands of men have died for reasons that were inextricably bound up with it. And yet among many other people on this earth, the word neither exists nor has any parallel because the concept is absent in their cultures. To substitute house or family would not convey what home means to us. For this reason translation from one language to another can sometimes be difficult. The difficulties become major ones where the languages represent cultures that have no traditions in common.

The problems involved are represented by the Polynesian word "mana." This word has overtones for the Polynesian that are beyond the experience of the European who has nothing among his own ideas to match it. It carries for Polynesians, among other things, the notion of a kind of power and virtue residing in certain individuals, animals or things, that is a sort of essence almost beyond control. It may be precious or sacred and require special care to preserve it from contamination. The very concept and the complex of ideas in which it is embedded are foreign to our way of thinking, lying altogether outside our culture. We consequently have no word to express it but must use the Polynesian one, just as we do taboo. Anthropologists have struggled for years to understand this word precisely and to comprehend fully its subtle overtones.

The word culture as I have been using it is somewhat parallel to all this. Until the concept it now represents, at least among anthropologists, was discovered, it could not enter into our thinking about ourselves, our way of life and our behavior. How far its value may extend can only be determined by testing it in various contexts. I am proposing here to apply certain aspects of cultural analysis, as formulated by anthropologists, to quite another way of thinking about ourselves, namely, history.[1]

There is a branch of history known as "culture history" which in the United States has a somewhat different significance from a similar word, *Kulturgeschichte,* in German. The Germans place in their culture history a much greater emphasis on literature and the arts. In this country we also include in this category not only these aspects of

[1] I am indebted to Dr. Donald Young for calling my attention to the report of the Committee on Historiography published by the Social Science Research Council, "The Social Sciences in Historical Study," Bulletin 64, 1954. I had already completed this section when the bulletin came to hand. It was, therefore, all the more gratifying to find myself in general agreement with the committee's suggestions for a fuller use of anthropology, as well as of other social sciences, by historians.

civilization, but studies, too, of less exalted activities and institutions, that are a more intimate part of everyday living. The country doctor, the storekeeper, modes of travel, and various other phases of life are subjects it has become customary for us to include in culture history.

This broadening of historical interests beyond the traditional ones is highly significant and reflects an important development, but it is not using culture in the fullest anthropological sense. Here we come face to face with the inconvenience of adopting for specialized usage a word which already has a wide currency in its own right. Since I am unable to suggest a substitute that is not awkward and contrived, I shall continue to use the word culture as I have defined it.

The essence of culture is pattern. This means that the whole is greater than the sum of its parts and, indeed, that the parts can be understood only in terms of the whole. Although for particular purposes an anthropologist may examine a single strand in a culture and compare it with similar ones in other cultures, he is always acutely aware that it is but a single strand. And the context into which it fits, the pattern it makes with other elements in the culture, is always a prime consideration. In an anthropological sense, then, a culture history should rest on the pattern of the culture as a whole—on its configuration, to use a synonym.

If history is to use culture in the anthropological sense, it must also be sensitive to the implications of process that are inherent in culture. Pattern is usually described in terms of a particular moment of time. Thus we may speak of the pattern of life in a feudal society and here we would have in mind, among other things, the kinds of institutions, the types of behavior, the prevailing ideas, the economy and the technology. To these we would add their special developments and their relations to one another, how one affected the other and the overall configuration they produced, making this culture distinct from all others. Such a description, however, would suggest a static balance, which hardly does justice to the concept of pattern as conceived by the anthropologist. In his view the pattern is a tendency rather than an accomplishment, the inherent balance *toward* which the various elements are moving but which they never quite reach. It is a becoming, for cultures are never perfectly balanced and fully achieved. The pattern, then, is a kind of process. Knowing this, the anthropologist can use pattern as a predictive tool under certain circumstances. He anticipates that such a pattern will mold and adjust new ideas to its prevailing configuration. Or conversely he may observe how new economic events, for example, may alter the pattern of a culture and thus alter the process it is following toward its fulfillment.

Process also enters into the anthropologist's consideration when he studies cultures in contact or conflict with each other. Under such circumstances patterns may be disturbed, they may reassert themselves in the same or a slightly different guise, or they may break up and new ones emerge. Less commonly he has a glimpse of the saturation of a pattern of culture, and for want of a better term, its renewal on a new process of development. Above all he is deeply aware of the continuity of change.

These concepts of pattern and process have been achieved largely by comparative methods. Anthropology, of all the social sciences, is by the nature of its subject matter committed to a world view and to comparison of one culture with another. Literally, seeking its subjects among primitive cultures, it found itself with material that had value only if it could be given broad application and if it yielded insights valid for broader perspectives than the obscure cultures themselves.

The natural curiosity about one's own antecedents, that can clothe simple narrative history with fascination, could scarcely be claimed for the people investigated by anthropologists. Who would have the interest and the time to read a learned and exhaustive history of the Bemba, for example, if it were written, as most of our national histories are, in purely local and narrative form? But if Bemba culture and experience throw light on the nature of culture in general, the way it develops and grows, and the functions and relationships of the various components in all culture, then the Bemba can provide significant data worth any scholar's time and effort. But this can only be determined by the careful assemblage of many cultures and by the comparison of one with the other. And this is precisely what anthropology in particular has done. It is therefore possible for anthropology to admit the uniqueness of each culture from an historical point of view, and yet to see in all cultures manifestation of common tendencies and principles, thus building up a corpus of theory which has broad and valid significance for our own society. These, then, are the reasons that have prompted me to differentiate between culture history, as now commonly understood, and the kind of culture history that might arise from the use of culture concepts elaborated by anthropology.

Culture, as an anthropologist sees it, and history are not ordinarily associated in our minds. And perhaps on first thought they would seem to have little if anything to do with each other. Although it is risky to generalize on a literature as vast as history's, I venture to say that few historians exhibit any familiarity whatever in their writing with the principles that anthropologists have been able to extract from cultural data. It is true, of course, that they have become increasingly aware of culture content; they could scarcely be historians without being up to their ears in some aspect of culture. But this is quite another matter from the application to history of generalizations based on cultural processes.

I suspect that part of the answer lies in the relatively recent discovery of culture, and the still more recent formulations that have grown out of anthropological investigations, for history has always shown in its own development considerable sensitivity to the intellectual and even the cultural patterns of the times. Its preoccupation with the Church and with little else from the time of St. Augustine, at the end of the fourth century, to the Magdeburg Centuries of the Age of the Reformation, fits in with the overwhelming role the Church played in the culture of that period. Other formative sources of modern history were the annals and chronicles of the monasteries, where again churchly affairs occupy many of the entries. The aristocratic traditions of feudalism were also reflected in the growing references in these chronicles to the exploits of the nobility. But this phase of feudal life is more strikingly mirrored in the almost exclusive attention the bards paid to the deeds of daring, conquests, loves and tragedies of the ruling classes. This, too, was a kind of history, albeit an oral one. It is tempting to attribute to these origins the long fixation of historians on kings and queens, even when their power had long vanished and after some of them were becoming aware that what counted in history often was little affected by royal or other aristocratic personages. But tradition dies hard. Carlyle gave it another twist with his theory of the role of the hero in history.

The influence of the cultural milieu on history

is nowhere more clearly evident than in the remarkable works of Machiavelli. Living in mid-
Renaissance when secular power was assuming a
dominant and brilliant role, his writing recognized
this profound change in society and helped to set
new and wider limits for historical inquiry. The
re-emergence of antiquity which began in the Renaissance and continued to affect European ideas
for the next four hundred years or more also found
its counterpart in an historical interest that produced Gibbon's monumental achievement. The
French Revolution with its focus on constitutions
began a trend that we now know as constitutional
history. Nationalism in the nineteenth century and
the economic struggles of the Age of Industrialization similarly stimulated among historians inquir-
ies in these fields. Histories of art, literature, architecture and science have each reflected similar
trends. The list might be lengthened still further,
but it is long enough to show the steady and constant tendency of history to widen its scope and embrace more and more of the institutions of
civilization.

Although history has enormously expanded its
interests, it has still remained for many of its practitioners a form of narrative art. The inherent

drama of personalities, their struggles for political power, the growth of institutions and the development of nations provided justification enough for their skill. How many histories, for example, have we read of the nineteenth century in England in terms of ministries, political maneuvers, kings and queens, wars and generals! The more venturesome occasionally add a grudging chapter or two on the arts and literature, or even a glimpse of economic conditions. And even the multi-volumed compendia, with contributions from all manner of specialized scholars covering a wide variety of topics, present a veritable feast that no one seems to be able to digest. With all this historical research, the fundamental cultural processes which were under way in England, and which have revolutionized the country's way of life more profoundly than a bloody civil war could have done, are virtually ignored.

The fact is that history has been guided in its development by two distinct and opposite forces. On the one hand, there is the literary tradition which has produced some of the enduring masterpieces of Western civilization. Tacitus, Thucydides, Herodotus, Gibbon take their places among the great in literature as well as in history. This tradition remains today a dominant factor. It has little or no scientific interest in history and one of its protagonists, the late James Harvey Robinson, declared that history should not even entertain such ambitions since by its very nature it could not be treated scientifically. In part this view rests on the belief, probably correct, that historical truth can be only approximate, at best, and that absolute truth is beyond the power of the historian. And it also rejects science on the grounds that it is incompatible with the unique nature of history. Edouard Meyer was of the opinion, shared by most historians, that each history represented a continuity of events in a causal relationship. As Vico, the great Italian historian, put it, each period is the seedbed of its successor. It follows, therefore, that each history is *sui generis,* unlike any other; in short, unique. Although we commonly say that history repeats itself, the historian in this tradition does not appear to believe it. He sees each historical sequence as distinct from all others and therefore not strictly comparable to them. Since science depends upon the repetition of events and the ability to compare one with another, history would seem outside its ministrations.

The other influence on history has been the

frank use of historical data to prove a thesis. This is nothing new, although it is sometimes made to seem as if it were. In recent times there have been notable efforts along these lines. Karl Marx in *Das Kapital,* for example, interpreted economic and social data to develop history for revolutionary and social action. There have been other attempts of this sort, but few of them have been either objective or scientific, and they have served to give scientific history a bad reputation.

CULTURE CONFLICT IN IRELAND

That some historians have become sensitive to the significance of cultural data, as the widening nets of historical research in history bring in more and more strange fish never previously considered digestible for historians stomachs or even pleasing to their palates, is becoming evident in the work of some recent writers. One example that is tailor-made for my argument is the highly perceptive account of the English efforts to conquer Ireland in the Age of Elizabeth which A. L. Rowse has recently published. In his book, *The Expansion of Elizabethan England,* Rowse combines a nice literary and historical appreciation of the personalities of the times with a vivid feeling for place and culture. In part, this seems to have developed from his earlier preoccupation with Cornwall, of which he is a native. To render the essential character of Cornwall one would inevitably need to compare it with the rest of England, to consider the reasons for Cornwall's difference, and to savor the survivals of the local culture that give this region its special flavor. At any rate, Rowse is to a noteworthy degree sensitive to cultural factors in history. In the following characterization of Ireland, I am borrowing heavily from him.

To illustrate one of the ways history can make use of anthropological experience, the conflict between the English and the Irish serves as an excellent example. The situation has many of the classic features of culture conflict, a phenomenon well known to anthropologists, who by comparative observations have been able to discern common tendencies, wherever it occurs. The events in Ireland, seen from this perspective, take on a far deeper meaning and provide a more convincing explanation of their eventual resolution than the standard narrative can give.

In the sixteenth century the gulf between England and Ireland was rapidly widening. England, in the course of the preceding four hundred or five hundred years, had been going through a profound reorganization of her social and cultural structure. And at the same time she had been achieving a political unity and centralization that contributed heavily to the direction and rapidity of the change. The enrichment and expansion of the economy had brought growing wealth to the realm and at the same time, by stimulating trade and commerce, opened the country to greater communication within, as well as outside, its borders. In short, England was becoming a modern nation, achieving a new pattern of civilization, and beginning to enjoy flexing the new muscles that all these changes had developed. The exuberance and the sense of power that generally accompany the initial stages of a new cycle were richly manifested in the extraordinary energy that characterized the Age of Elizabeth. We see the same thing in a slightly earlier period in Italy. It appears time after time in China. In our own world, it is plain to recognize in the United States and in Russia.

A little less than four hundred years ago in England this cultural energy burst forth in a remarkable literature, a brilliant society and an unprecedented maritime activity. The fabulous success of the Spaniards and the Portuguese in acquiring new territory, establishing trade routes and taking possession of unearned increments wherever they could, aroused in the highly activated English a strong degree of envy and a desire to get in on the ground floor. The Elizabethan Englishmen were looking in various directions for new worlds to conquer. Just across a narrow channel lay Ireland where the contrast with all this could scarcely have been greater. Ireland had virtually a Neolithic culture, with some overtones of Bronze and Iron age technological developments. Fundamentally, its life was laid out along lines similar to those of other Celtic people which means, among other things, a clan or lineage organization of society. The clans, called *septs* in Ireland, owned the land and it was through membership in one of them that the individual Irishman had any rights to it. He could neither sell nor buy the land he used. And the chieftain had no more right to do so than any other member of the clan. He had only a life tenure and his personal rights did not extend beyond his personal desmesne. Such notions of property were a far cry from private ownership or the extensive powers of the lord of the manor familiar to the English.

The economy, too, was quite unlike the settled agricultural world that had developed in England. The warm, tight village life of the English country-side had no counterpart in Ireland. Instead the people led a kind of migratory pastoral existence, with the whole community following their cattle to the mountains for summer pasturage. Cows represented wealth and passed for currency. In such a primitive and semi-communal society, there were no neat farms with tidy steadings, no tenantry paying rents to landlords, no taxes to fill the coffers of government and no officials to put their hands into such coffers. The English found all this a barbarous life and unbelievaly primitive. "No historian," declares Rowse, "has brought home how different a world Ireland was." No historian, in fact, until Rowse had really sensed the significance of these cultural factors in shaping the events that were to follow these Elizabethan contacts.

The motivations of the Irish were also difficult for the English to comprehend, since they arose from cultural conditions utterly foreign to them. Time and again the Irish leaders seemed wholly unpredictable, willful and unreliable. Promises and agreements were made but not kept and courses of action were followed that confounded the English. The misunderstanding on this score often arose from the fact that the power of the Irish leader was based on quite a different system from that of the English. The clan leader in Ireland did not inherit his position. He was chosen by the clan from its leading family by the ancient law of tanistry. His power, therefore, was derived from the consent of the clan and his continuance as leader depended on the support of his clansmen. He was far from being the hereditary, arbitrary and powerful lord that the English projected from their own experience. Frequently therefore his actions would be determined by matters of clan policy beyond the ken of the English.

On the point of manners and customs the two people were miles apart. In fact, the English were shocked by what they called the "incivility" of the Irish, by which they meant the lack of refinement in manners and customs and the appearance of barbarism in their way of life. They lived in hovels, they wore strange costumes and dressed their hair in long *glibs* which made disguise easy. They drew blood from living cows and used it for food

—a practice that seemed particularly revolting to English observers. They quartered their animals with themselves. Their husbandry was unbelievably primitive and inefficient. And this same backwardness was apparent even in their arms. Battle axes were of Norse vintage and the native kerne fought without armor, employing outmoded short bows, round shields and darts.

If all this were not enough, the Irish seemed inefficient and lazy. In spite of their Christianity, they were given to magic practices, survivals of an earlier and still more primitive society. Concubinage, among other sexual customs, was widely tolerated. It is curious to note that the sexual laxness from which the English might have been expected to obtain some comfort was also condemned.

Living as they did in a simple economy, dependent on their cattle, in a virtual subsistence on their own resources, it is hardly to be expected that the Irish would have developed any considerable degree of trade either internally between various parts of the island or with other countries. Under these conditions, roads were few and in an abominable state. Many districts were even cut off from any easy or regular communication with one another. The Lord Deputy Chichester wrote of Ulster that "before these last wars it was as inaccessible to strangers as the Kingdom of China." And Rowse describes this region as "cut off as it had been from prehistoric times from the rest of Ireland behind its barriers of lakes, bogs, and rivers." It was the most Celtic part of Ireland, where the culture equivalent to an outmoded one long vanished in England itself had lingered on in the peripheral regions of Ireland and Scotland.

Of some significance in this picture were the bards. Long since vanished from England, they remained an important element in the remnants of the Celtic world wherever it survived. As repositories of the ancient oral literature of their people, they kept alive the epics and the balladry of Ireland. Although Rowse characterizes Irish literature as stagnant at this time, it was nevertheless a living and vital part of Irish life. And more important it was in its way a common expression of the people as a whole. Embodied in it were the pride, the glory, the tragedies and the hopes of the Irish themselves. The bards, therefore, were a rallying point of patriotism and a focus for the feeling of communion as one people. That the ballads and the epics were in Erse made them all the more an Irish possession distinct from anything English.

Into this society of "dissolution" and "decay" that was unable to form a national, modern state on the basis of its own existing institutions and culture pattern, the English flung themselves in the reign of Elizabeth as in that of her father Henry before her. Rowse considers this aggression inevitable in the logic of events. England had become a highly successful national state, efficient, energetic and fulfilling the pattern she had been gradually developing. Not only was this energy turning into channels obvious from geographic propinquity, but of more vital concern to England's survival in the highly competitive and throat-cutting world of international rivalry, Ireland's conquest, or at least her neutralization, was essential. Spain, with her powerful navy and her desire to crush the threat of upstart England, more than once had considered Ireland to be England's soft underbelly. French intrigue was also an ever present danger here, as it was later in Scotland.

How much the religious defection of England from Rome left Ireland more solidly aligned with potential Catholic enemies is a moot point, but it is clear from any reading of history that religion and religious affiliations could play a far greater role in the affairs of Europe in the sixteenth century than in our times. The conflicts of religion were still fresh and there were more to come before men would cease to align themselves in European wars on religious grounds. For such reasons, as well as, I suppose, the opportunities for younger sons and other adventurers seeking to establish themselves, Ireland seemed a natural target for English enterprise.

And what about Ireland? Had she evolved *pari passu* with the modernization of Europe and achieved the cultural revolution that would have permitted the growth of a centralized national state, it is most unlikely that Elizabeth would have ventured to send armies to conquer her. The Queen was far too cautious and shrewd a statesman, in the face of obvious dangers in other directions, to risk the kind of total war that this conquest would have taken. With her forces and wealth engaged in such a struggle, she would have been an easy victim for her enemies. That she knew this is clear from her unwillingness ever to commit herself too deeply in Ireland. Indeed, one of the constant complaints of her generals and representatives in the Irish wars is on the score of her unwillingness to go all out on this venture. Actually, much of the time she could not do so, since she was busily keeping her continental rivals from her shores or was fully occupied elsewhere. That, too, took money, men and generals. She hoped to reduce Ireland "on the cheap."

The clash, then, between England and Ireland was not too different in its elements from the conflicts between European colonial powers and the native cultures they have attempted to dominate. In the consequences of such an attempt to dominate Ireland, we see all too tragically played out before us the story that was to be repeated over and over again elsewhere in the next four hundred years with substantially the same results. Ireland happens to be one of the earliest examples in modern times of culture conflict and an almost classic example of the genre. But the British in India, the French in North Africa, the Dutch in Java, have re-enacted the theme with local trimmings.

Although the English finally managed to conquer Ireland in a military way and to sequestrate large land holdings for the benefit of English settlers, many of whom were actually Welsh and Cornishmen, they never really subdued the people or persuaded them to adopt the English way of life. The English failed in this because they never fully appreciated the profound influence that culture exerts on the motivations and attitudes of a people, nor realized how powerfully people in these circumstances react. It was this inability to envision, let alone to dissolve, the conflicts of culture that finally proved to be the rock on which the English venture in Ireland foundered. By the time England had become conciliatory, the pattern of resistance had hardened. Ireland had to be released and culture had triumphed.

But the culture of Ireland had been altered in the process. The conflict almost at once began to throw certain aspects of Irish life into greater prominence. The bards, for example, became centers of resistance. By employing traditional and accepted routes to Irish emotion they were able to intensify tribal loyalties and raise local patriotism to a high degree of fervor.

The Church itself, long established and for centuries maintaining a kind of autonomy, underwent a profound revivification. Rowse describes the condition of the Church prior to English invasion as deplorable. It was, he says, moribund, lax and corrupt. Generally the observances were perfunctory and external. The cathedrals, not to speak of the local churches, were in sad states of dilapidation. Of 224 parishes, only 52 were at all regularly served by permanent vicars. And 105 churches, together with their lands, were simply leased out to farmers and their religious functions abandoned. No wonder the English spoke of the widespread laxness in marriage and the practice of open concubinage.

With the invasion of the English, all this changed. At least, the Church became a pillar of Irish nationalism. As an institution in Irish life, it grew into a pivotal position, becoming in fact the only national institution where control was wholly Irish and thus symbolizing the unity of the people. The high degree of integration of Irish life with the Church, which has always seemed so characteristic of Ireland, now appears as the consequence of English pressures.

This development is not so very different from anthropological experience with primitive cultures under duress from European civilization and where their own patterns of living are seriously threatened. Here, too, religious phenomena are characteristic expressions as part of a rebirth of "nativism." Old cults are revived in new guises, or new emotional religious developments flourish, and serve as points of reorientation or adaptation to the experiences the people are undergoing. People who find their old, cherished and comfortable ways of life threatened with dissolution and are facing the uncertainties of new, untried and uncongenial practices react either with feelings of despair or with vigorous efforts to save what they can, even if it requires some adjustment in the saving.

One wonders whether or not the strong emotional and spiritual meaning of the Church for other European minorities, similarly under pressures such as the Irish endured, also sprang from the same reactions. At least one observes that the life of the people and the Church were more closely integrated in Poland where cultural oppression or cultural resentment existed than in other areas where these feelings were absent or minor. It is, moreover, a common observation that religion among the Jews has loosened its hold to the extent that cultural disabilities against them have ameliorated.

It would take us too far afield to discuss in more detail or to analyze more fully the history of Ireland from the sixteenth century to our own. And there are still many fascinating facets of these fateful centuries that I have altogether omitted mentioning. I am, for example, not even touching on the timing of the processes of reaction, and I have only suggested the thought that with all the resistance of the culture under attack, some deposits are left by the invading culture. The conflict is never a negative process.

History written from these premises offers a richer understanding of the ground swells of historical events than do the mere accounts of battles fought, personal ambitions achieved or thwarted, or political manipulations frustrated or consummated. In the case of Ireland, to write of these transitory events, without the interpretation that cultural processes make possible, would be like describing the production of fire from steel on flint and mentioning the sparks but forgetting the agents. But no, this is perhaps not quite an accurate simile. History can be more complex than this. Sometimes the events shaped by cultural process can themselves affect culture itself.

CULTURE IN AMERICAN HISTORY

Although there are many other examples of the part that cultural dynamics plays in history, deep below the surface of personalities and political activity, I shall have time to refer to only one other. And this one is from our own annals.

The role of cultural process in determining history is perhaps nowhere clearer, or shall I say more readily recognizable, than in the history of the United States. And although most writers on the subject have followed conventional patterns in narrating the events of our past by emphasizing what Charles Beard has called "barren 'political' history," there have nevertheless been an important number of historians in this country who have been sensitive to cultural factors. Perhaps the first of them to appreciate fully the value of cultural interpretations was Turner, in his now classic study of the effect of the frontier culture patterns upon Americans politics.

One cannot help wondering whether this very recognition in this country may not be attributable to the fact that the United States is a new nation, in which the problems of adapting European traditions to the American environment have been an especially prominent feature in our consciousness. Because of this, Americans generally are rather more aware than Europeans of such cultural undercurrents. Also, as a nation made up of a variety of ethnic strains, each with its own peculiar culture and often distinct language, we have somehow felt more vividly the play of culture contact, ac-

culturation and other cultural processes going on
in our daily lives and affecting our behavior. So
that even if many of us have only sensed these
things deeply, without conceptualizing them or giving them names, we are quick to recognize their
reality once they are generalized for us. Europeans
living in a world of greater cultural maturity are
less likely to be as sensitive to them. Moreover the
comparable developments in Europe achieved their
essential resolutions at a time when historical interest was more narrowly focused and society was
less articulate on such matters.

But the frontier, important as it was, was not
the only cultural pattern expressing itself in American life or in our history. Who does not know the
significance of minority and nationality blocs in
our practical politics? How often have we talked
about the Irish vote, the Italian, Polish, and more
recently the Negro vote? Constantly we see how
such groups of votes are courted by politicians,
how they influence decisions on national and sometimes international affairs. It is a phenomenon that
is peculiarly American and has had a far greater
effect on our history than our textbooks would suggest.

Although some writers have recognized the influence that this pattern of voting has exercised in politics, I am unaware of any detailed consideration by an historian of its emergence among us on cultural grounds.[1] And yet this, it strikes me, is where it begins and why it developed. Historians have left to the anthropologist and the sociologist the analysis of the cultural dislocations accompanying the immigration and settlement of various national and ethnic groups in the United States. These social scientists have produced a considerable literature on the effects of the process of acculturation that immigration brings in its train and which has been going on from our beginnings but more particularly during the nineteenth and twentieth centuries. They have amassed impressive evidence on the development of patterns of minority or group feeling. They have shown how these groups evolve as subcultures within the national culture and make loyalties of their own that can exist and accommodate themselves in most cases to the larger loyalty to country—but not always. By appealing to the special interests, the special loyalties or the special insecurities of such groups, clever

[1] The recent work of Handlin, Wittke and others reveals a growing appreciation of this phase of our history and a closer approach to a cultural orientation than historians have generally shown.

politicians have been able to use them for their
purposes.

Sectionalism is another national characteristic
well known in our history, in fact, one that was
responsible for the most serious threat to our fed-
eral existence. Purely political commentary on its
rise has never appeared adequate as an explanation
for its appearance in our society. With the recognition of economics as a potent factor in directing
the course of political events, interpretations along
these lines were applied to sectionalism as well as
to many other developments in our history. Frequently this has led to a clearer understanding of
the influences underlying them. We are coming to
realize that important as economic factors may be,
they are not the only ones, particularly in the kind
of broad cultural adaptations that sectionalism represents. For sectionalism involves more than plan-
tation economy versus industrialization or the demand for a high tariff. Strong as the motives for
economic protection or preferment may be in guid-
ing political measures and undeniable as they are
in such situations, sectionalism also represents the
adaptation of cultural patterns and values to the
environment and the growth of traditions and customs peculiar to a special region. The pride of a

Southerner is a defense of a way of life, not of an economic doctrine. The New Englander feels himself part of a tradition that is far greater than the needs of an industrial system. The special features that characterize the life of the Northwest are rooted in richer soil than the interests of the lumberman or the orchardist. These subtle differentiations, so hard sometimes to define, but so patent to an American, lend color to our national culture, create variety of point of view and sometimes affect major issues. It is not an idle question to ask whether the attitudes of the Middle West, shaped by its geographic position and its local institutions, did not affect the date of our entry in World Wars I and II.

Even the preservation of the shape and the organization of our original colonies in a union of states, thus creating a novel form of government, reflects the sectionalism that had already evolved when the Union was established. In those days a man was a Virginian or a Massachusetts man before he was anything else. So deep ran these feelings that a united country would have been impossible without taking them into account. Our very form of government is a product of colonial traditions preserved in our states.

We have all been raised to regard the Declaration of Independence and the Constitution of the United States as noble documents. And I think we are plainly justified in that belief. Certainly it has been supported by many acute students from other countries who have had no special axe to grind in commending them. Among the things frequently mentioned to their great distinction is that they were the *creation* of exceptionally gifted men. That a relatively few men could have summoned up out of their wisdom documents that so fitted the needs and so reflected the ideals of a new, untried and unorganized collection of colonies and would serve them so well and, on the whole, so efficiently for close to two hundred years, often seems in retrospect miraculous. I trust I will not be put down as subversive if I suggest that with all deference to the perspicacity of the founders, some of their utterances and many of their provisions could not have been said or set forth in any other country or in any other culture than the one in which they found themselves.

Already, by 1776, after one hundred and fifty years of settlement and adaptation in the New World, the cultural characteristics of the Colonial Americans had perceptibly deviated from the parent culture, from which most of the colonists were removed by several generations. The class structure, for example, of England was becoming more and more rigid while in America it was dissolving under the influence of the more primitive conditions of a young society and of a pioneering world. The dependence of settlers in virgin country on their own resources and at the same time the development under these circumstances of a greater degree of cooperation made the inflexibility of the older system unworkable. Moreover, the economic fluidity and the more rapid rise and descent in the economic scale offered little foundation for a class structure such as existed in the Old World. Thus social distinctions between men were nominal, and when they existed in embryo they had not gone far enough to eradicate the notion that one man was as good as another. Too many had risen within one lifetime to prominent positions to allow discouragement of this widely held democratic belief.

Liberty, freedom and independence were words the founders used over and over. They were not empty symbols to whip up enthusiasm, but living realities to most of the colonists, who enjoyed these blessings in their daily lives. In their remote settlements, they saw few officials and experienced little or no interference with their habits and practices, which were derived from immediate and practical necessities. Independent action and enterprise were essential if these families were to survive, let alone flourish. Thus there grew up traditions of looking to their own efforts to solve their problems, of taking action without waiting for bureaucratic responsibility to move and of a detestation of interference from outside. These are traits that generally emerge among pioneering people who are burdened by a minimum of cultural baggage and are actually forging a cultural tradition of their own.

It is therefore not surprising that at the very outset the Declaration of Independence states that all men are created equal. This was an *ideal* of our colonial society, so firmly established that even if some of the signers may not have personally subscribed to it, they would not have ventured to denounce it publicly. Our own faith and conviction in democracy as a way of life similarly represents a collective *ideal* of our culture even though there may be some who hold other ideas. It would take a very courageous public figure, not to say a foolish one, to deny what the people cherish. Thus, the fact that some of the signers were men of social prestige and fortune and might have been expected to favor more class consciousness simply demonstrates the power of a cultural ideal.

Repeatedly the Bill of Particulars setting forth the grievances of the colonists mentions British actions without their consent. Here is a reflection of a profound irritation that springs directly from the habit and custom of the colonists to manage their own affairs and a refusal to brook interference. Where could this attitude have come from? The taxations were not altogether unjust; the regulation of commerce and trade by the mother country was common policy in Spain, France, Portugal and the Netherlands. It is true that a parliamentary system existed in the traditions of the colonists brought from Britain, but it was a system that had not yet developed into its present form and did not then permeate the political activity of the mass of people. Undoubtedly the seeds of representative government we owe to Britain, but the germination and growth of the plant itself we can claim as the production of the social and cultural conditions that arose in America. Any comparison of the British system with our own reveals distinct differences that could have emerged only from such circumstances.

It seems ironic in our time to note that the colonists objected to "swarms of officials." Certainly this was a revulsion natural to a people accustomed to a pioneering life. What they would have thought of the vast numbers of officials that were to be home-grown is not hard to fancy. One also notes that standing armies seemed in those days completely distasteful and foreign. This national bias has lasted until quite recently.

This is not the place to pursue in more detail other evidences of the influence of cultural pattern on the form and character of our establishing documents, but I cannot pass on without reference to the pervasive efforts to secure liberty and freedom for the individual that are so clearly manifest in the Constitution itself, nor fail to reflect on the incorporation into the Union of the various colonies as distinct states, whose rights were carefully defined and whose diverse identities were preserved. One could for administrative purposes have devised more efficient political divisions and more centralized control. But it was precisely this that would have destroyed local loyalties and cultural patterns and, incidentally, made the Union impossible. It had to be on the terms set by colonial patterns or not at all.

History, if it is to recreate our past, has to take account of all the significant factors responsible for it. Thus in its development history has found itself required to expand its researches and widen its vision as new orientations and new sources of insight become accessible. To advocate pursuit of these new lines of inquiry does not by any means suggest abandonment of the old. The task, therefore, becomes progressively more and more formidable, and the historian may well quail before it. The solution, in spite of this, is not less history, but more of it and the kind of specialization that now exists. We need historical scholars trained in specialties which will enable them to bring the values they possess to the sum total of history in forms available for synthesis. If the researches of historians of economics, of science, of art, of literature, of ideas and of various other aspects of our civilization have proved fruitful, as few will deny, then might we not expect that at the least the anthropological study of our history would also bring deeper insights? For anthropology by its cultural orientation is more likely to provide the kinds of tools and the concepts that would reveal the way in which our patterns of living and our cultural processes shape our institutions and control our history.

However much this kind of contribution might lend to historical understanding, it still remains in the tradition of narration. Implicit in this is the uniqueness of the event and its chain of cause and effect. History has in the main avoided any guise of science—any attempt to generalize from the events it describes. But anthropological method and experience point to another contribution they can offer to history. Although anthropology recognizes the unique nature of any culture and the path of its development, it has come to see that similarities of cultural reaction can also be identified and that generalizations may be drawn from the comparative study of a large number of different cultures. It has identified certain processes that can, I think, be useful in historical analysis and suggests that the comparative method has a distinct value for history.

3 RECOVERY OF THE PAST

One of the most remarkable achievements of man is the way he has managed to recover his past from the unpromising relics of ages long forgotten and by this to gain a perspective of himself in time. This, it strikes me, has never been properly valued as an intellectual achievement or for the insight it provides man in one of his chief occupations—studying himself. We are all properly impressed by the astounding results of scientific research into the nature of the physical world around us; we appreciate and benefit directly from investigations into the functioning of our bodies as organisms. We

pay tribute to the indefatigable spirit that has led
man to explore his geography, forging into every
nook and cranny of it. But man's ability to push
back the curtains obscuring his past is a less obvious
accomplishment than these, and its meaning can be
grasped only from the revolutionary change it has
created in our understanding of the nature and
origin of man and his civilization.

It is hard for us, accustomed to modern concepts
of space and time, to realize how narrow the vistas
of past ages were in both these respects. Herodotus,
one of the most widely traveled and erudite men
of his time, knew the world bordering the Mediterranean and, in certain areas, some distance back
from its shores. China and the East, however, were
beyond his ken. Africa below the Sahara was unknown to him. All of northern and western Europe
represented a vague and uncertain region. And of
course the New World was not to be discovered for
another two thousand years or so. Yet constricted as
this knowledge of the physical world seems to us, it
did embrace all of one of the great centers of civilization [1] where some of the loftiest peaks of the human mind were being attained. And by contrast

[1] I am recognizing at this point in history China and India, in
addition to the Mediterranean, as foci of high civilizations.

with what was known of man in time, it was considerable.

But what did Herodotus, or any other literate Athenian, know of the past and the reaches of time? Herodotus lived in the fifth century B.C. and to Athenians of that time, even Homer, who had lived only four or five hundred years before, had become scarcely more than a name. The heroes of the Iliad, described by Homer several hundred years after their eventful careers, were vivid enough, but back of that everything faded into a legendary and timeless world. I hesitate to suggest a precise time limitation to Herodotus' vision into the past since he was aware of Egypt's antiquity and of the fact that Asia Minor and even Hellas itself had some historical depth, but I doubt if his knowledge carried him back much beyond one or two thousand years.

That the Greeks were ever very much concerned with this problem is not very clear. The question of the origin of man and how he arrived at his present level of civilization seems not to have troubled them much, if at all. Their mythology, by providing a cosmogenesis of sorts, dulled to some extent the edge of any serious queries they might have had along these lines. Just as culture offered no sustained challenge to their inquiring minds because they had not yet discovered the nature of it, so perhaps for the same reason they were not puzzled about human origins and the growth of civilization.

The span of two thousand years of historical depth that we might generously allow Herodotus is but a minute fraction of man's history on this planet and an infinitesimal fraction of the history of the planet itself. If we take the age of the earth as three and one-half billion years [2] and man's first appearance on it as one million years ago, then Herodotus' view, dim as it was, could only carry him back into the earth's past 6/100,000 of 1 per cent of the way and, as far as human history goes, 2/10 of 1 per cent. These comparisons are not, of course, to be taken too literally, but they do illustrate how limited a view a Greek of one of the most luminous periods in the history of man could take of the long, arduous road that mankind had traveled. By this very fact he was cut off from an appreciation of what his past signified in itself and what it had to say as to his present and future.

[2] This is a conservative estimate extended by some scientists to five billion years.

If this was all the Greeks could recover of their past, their contemporaries and predecessors obviously could do no better and probably much worse. The Hebrews were a possible exception since the Bible carried their history back several millennia, but beyond that there was only the void.

This limitation of perspective continued until quite recently except as time itself accumulated and added to what the Greeks and Hebrews already knew, or thought they knew, of the past. Even as late as the end of the eighteenth century most scholars followed Bishop Ussher in dating the beginning of the world at 4004 B.C., and considered real history to begin with the Greeks. Ancient civilizations long forgotten still lay mouldering in the ground while their architectural remains bore silent witness to the observation that men have eyes but they see not. As for those still earlier cultures and the evidences of the crude beginnings of mankind, they continued to be turned up by the peasant's plow and to be discarded as of no special interest. The polished stone tools accidentally unearthed were simply regarded as thunderbolts hurled from the sky and turned to stone. The fanciful conceit of Lucretius that men once used stone for tools before they learned to fashion metal, suggesting ages long past and forgotten, seemed too farfetched to be taken seriously.

With the beginning of the nineteenth century, scholars like Layard began to be interested in the unexplained ruins of Asia Minor, and enthusiastic amateurs like Boucher de Perthes were starting collections of shaped stones that they were recognizing as the tools of primitive men. Darwin startled the mid-nineteenth-century world with a view that man might have a somewhat more ancient organic lineage than had been previously conceded him. Slowly at first, but with quickening tempo, the relics of man's past in the shape of his bones and the imperishable products of his hands have been unearthed. And trained scholars have become amazingly adept at squeezing out more and more information from such refractory material. Thus in little over a century a vast world was discovered— the world from which our civilization had emerged, and, like a cocoon abandoned by a butterfly, it had forgotten. This vast world was a new world, and yet one as old as man himself. Now for the first time man could look back and get some notion, however uncertain in spots, of the road he had traversed and the time it had taken.

THE ORIGIN OF CIVILIZATION

It has become apparent that the kind of life we lead —what we call civilized and appropriately named from the Latin *civilis*, or citified—is quite new in the history of mankind. The identification of civilization with cities is based on sound principle and ample evidence. No civilization has ever arisen without cities, for cities are indispensable when the economy becomes rich and complex enough to support civilization.[3] During the long ages when man was a hunter, a fisherman or a food gatherer— all during the Paleolithic in fact—his economy did not permit large aggregations of people in one area and was therefore incapable of supporting civilization. It has been roughly estimated that on the average it takes ten square miles to support one

[3] I am taking here a higher, if narrower, standard of civilization than Toynbee, for example. He includes in his now famous, many-volumed *A Study of History*, the Eskimo, Polynesian, nomadic and early Irish cultures as examples of civilization. None of these had cities in a true sense, but neither were they civilizations. At the most, one can say that certain promising creative impulses were active in early Ireland and Polynesia, and that the Eskimo were highly ingenious (no doubt they had to be to survive). But if Eskimo and Polynesians are to be included as civilizations, then why not the Northwest Coast cultures, the African kingdoms, the pueblos of the Southwest and various other cultures? My view, I suppose, is that the precipitating factor is an economic one.

person in a hunting society and of course much more area than this where the resources are scanty. Thus a hunting family of five or six would require many times the land that would be needed by a farming unit of the same size. This meant, of course, that populations existing on such an economy were thin and distances between them great. Each unit had to be self-sufficient and trained in those skills necessary to maintain life. Each hunter caught all his food and made all his equipment. Life was necessarily simple and nomadic to some extent.

The introduction of agriculture in the Neolithic began to break up this ancient self-sufficiency, but not completely. Farming even on a very primitive level and with low production appeared only eight or ten thousand years ago at the outside. It brought many changes, but in particular it meant that life had to become sedentary. Each family was necessarily tied to its land if it was to harvest the fruits of its toil and if it was to use a field another year. Sedentary life also encouraged more permanent dwellings. Now it was worthwhile, in the greater comfort achieved, to put effort into building homes that would be used for more than a brief season. Finer stone tools were needed for carpentry; pottery was feasible when household goods were not a constant burden to be transported from one place to another; looms and woven goods were substituted for the skins of animals no longer hunted or even available, where the land was opened up for agriculture. The Neolithic settlements excavated by archaeologists reveal an appreciable increase in the concentration of population. Small villages now appeared, but no cities. Life, however, still remained on a largely subsistence basis; each family producing for its own needs. The surpluses available in this new system of economy were small, but apparently large enough to support some markets and to encourage some specialization of labor.

Not until the discovery of metals, however, did the economy advance to the point where surpluses were substantial. With them some men could pay others to do certain specialized tasks for them. These workers, or artisans, receiving their support in this manner, could live in towns since their labor no longer was in the fields. Moreover, as the farmers acquired wealth and grew in number, they not only needed protection from the raiding groups surrounding them, but also a social system that could regulate the more complex relationships that concentration of people brings in its train. All this required a centralization that made towns a necessity as well as a convenience. They became centers of defense, government, religion, trade and industry. As prototypes of the city they first appear in the Copper and early Bronze Age somewhere around 3500 B.C., or roughly fifty-five hundred years ago. This is the beginning of what Professor Childe has called the "urban revolution" and it is the beginning in all its essential features of what we know as civilization. From this point on, the anonymity of the past begins to fade as specific people of known name and achievement take their places in history. We can identify certain developments as of Sumerian, Babylonian, Hittite or Egyptian origin. We know the names of some of the conquering tribes that played important roles in the sequences of civilization. History now has *dramatis personae*.

CYCLES OF CIVILIZATION

It is this appearance of the cast with their entrances and their exits, their rise to glory and their extinction, that now dramatizes a phenomenon widely held to be inherent in civilization itself. This is the tendency, indeed considered by some to be an inexorable law, for civilization to proceed on its course in cycles, pulsations or waves of high achievement, followed by dissolution, exhaustion or extinction. The words used to describe the process vary, but the general picture is the same— the very antithesis of a continuous, uninterrupted course.

These cycles have recently attracted renewed interest from Professor Toynbee's attempt to find in the history of all civilizations the regularities that explain them and that might permit us to meet, with some degree of insight and knowledge, the difficulties that beset our own civilization. Toynbee's analysis has a rigidity that some critics have found quite unacceptable. And although he has disowned the naive organic concept of Spengler, he has set up a sequence through which civilization passes that nevertheless suggests a similar inevitability. This view of civilization has received considerable acceptance since it reflects a widely held notion that our standard histories have done much to fix in our minds. It pictures civilization as having a birth, a childhood, a maturity, concluding with senescence and death. Although literary license is partly responsible for this presentation of history, it goes far beyond that in such interpretations as Spengler's, for example, where the contemporary civilization of Western Europe is described as following this predetermined organic cycle and as having now reached a senescence presaging death.

Among the difficulties that beset an analysis of this problem is the lack of precise and discriminating words at our command. We speak of French civilization and Western civilization when the one is merely a local phase of the other. And we have no name at all for the long, continuous tradition that, beginning in the Tigris-Euphrates valley, has managed to survive into our own day.

Besides this, our histories are generally written about nations. We have histories of the Greeks, the Hittites, the Egyptians, the Romans, and in our time of the French, the British, the Germans. Since the framework of such narratives is political, all else becomes subordinate to it, even civilization. Thus the cultural activities that flourished among the Hittites or in the Greek city states are treated as distinct civilizations, as though unrelated to their contemporaries and perishing with the loss of their political identities. This identification of a specific civilization with a nation creates confusion when we are speaking in terms of civilization apart from national or local manifestations of it, and it also reinforces the impression that extinction is the inescapable fate of all civilizations, because so many of the actors in the drama of civilization have vanished from the scenes.

But even when the course of civilization is defined, not in terms of the fortunes of a nation, but of its own development, we can still discern a cyclical progress. At first glance this seems different from the growth of the simpler cultures that preceded it. In the thousands, the hundreds of thousands, of years before the appearance of civilization, the development of culture appears to have followed a fairly steady course, with its technological adjuncts gradually increasing in variety, number and efficiency. We can trace in the remains of these ancient cultures the slowly perfected techniques of shaping stone, beginning with the crudest kind of chipping and ending with amazingly delicate and controlled methods. We see from time to time the addition of such inventions as weaving, pottery making, the wheel, domestication of plants and animals, various power-generating devices and a host of other inventions and refinements. Once achieved, none of these fundamental additions was lost, but they were permanently added to the growing accumulation of culture, enriching it, providing elements for new combinations and new inventions, and placing in man's hands the ability to use his environment more effectively than ever before. All this, as I have said, gives the impression of a straight line progression without the cyclic and pulsating character we associate with civilization.

I suspect that if we knew enough of the details of the more remote past, some of this undeviating development would break down into component phases that show some degree of pulsation. The appearance of steady progress is partly the effect of distance and the loss of detail. But not altogether, for if we examine primitive culture closely over a long-term span, the apparent rise and decline is generally more evident in the changes of pottery design, or some similar stylistic expression, than in actual evidence of a serious loss of techniques or descent from one level of culture to a lower one. Leaving aside the changes brought about by the replacement of one tradition by another, following conquest or ecological modifications, often what appears to be a retrogression may actually be a retooling to fit some change in economy. A high technical skill displayed in the execution of a tool might seem lost in the succeeding form. But this may be merely the adjustment that accompanies a change rather than a deterioration, just as our earliest automobiles, although technically an advance, were inferior esthetically in style and design to the best carriages that preceded them. This distinction, however, is one that has never been adequately examined or discussed by archaeologists and I may be overstressing the point.

The fact does remain, however, that once we reach the levels we call civilization, the cyclic nature of its development becomes a far more prominent feature than before. The questions we have to ask, then, are these: Is civilization divisible into a number of distinct, more or less unconnected episodes, each inevitably ending in extinction? Or is it a continuous process without a complete break, but undergoing continuous change?

In examining these questions it is important to recall a distinction I made earlier: the distinction between civilization and the particular national vessel that may contain a special part of the whole. This figure hardly does justice to the complexity of civilization and its varied expression. Any people rising from barbarity will borrow from the civilization that is most accessible to it, either by tradition or propinquity. What is borrowed may be converted into a local or national manifestation that has a character of its own, and in some cases even profoundly affect the main stream of the civilization of which it is a part. The destruction of such a national phase of a civilization does not mean that the whole tradition goes down with it, even though the loss may be a grievous one.

A clear differentiation should therefore be made between civilizations and their national phases. In the five or six thousand years that civilization has existed, a rather considerable number of nations or states have appeared and vanished not only in different places but following one another in the same place. Some of these have apparently lost their vitality as organized political entities and have perished, their particular expression of civilization along with them. Others, through no fault of their own, have been destroyed by some outside agency. Warfare on an important scale, it is evident from the archaeological evidence, enters the picture in the Neolithic when the early agriculturists began to provide by their labor and their surpluses attractive game for their neighbors. But it is only in the Metal ages, when civilization had finally matured, that warfare took on a more ominous development as a kind of organized business. By this time the material rewards for the victor had become enormous and the growth of population had begun to exert pressures of its own, introducing motives quite different from those inspiring the casual raids of tribesmen. Now, schemes of annihilation, conquest and slavery served to further the power ambitions of monarchs, to satisfy the needs of growing populations, and to furnish the labor that the increasingly complex economy demanded. Thus some of the centers of civilization, whose remains we are at present exhuming from the rubble of antiquity, may have been victims of the destructive force of outside agencies, and their addition to the ruins of the past may have been accidental rather than the result of an organic cycle leading to decay and extinction. But these fortunes of state, nation or empire should not be identified or confused with the civilization of which they are a part, and which may continue to flourish long after the political entities, through which civilization expresses itself, have been dissolved.

CONTINUITY OF CIVILIZATION

What happens, then, to civilizations apart from their manifestations in states or nations? Let us examine some of the longest-lived. Although the general impression exists that all civilizations eventually disappear, this is not necessarily true. In the Old World there were four distinct areas where civilization took early root and from which it eventually spread into surrounding regions, giving rise subsequently to new manifestations. These were Egypt, the Near East, India and China. The first two were probably the older and it seems likely were responsible for the diffusion of the technological advances that subsequently stimulated similar developments farther east.[4] Just as we find in plant distribution the greatest number of varieties close to the center of origin, so in the area of the Near East the greatest luxuriance of forms and types of civilization appears.

In the case of China, the development and continuity of her civilization has continued unbroken for approximately thirty-five hundred years. Dy-

[4] It is even possible, as Heine-Geldern has argued in "L'origine des anciennes civilizations" (*Diogène*, January, 1956), that civilization actually arose first in the Near East and spread from there to the other three major foci of development.

nasty followed dynasty, sometimes through internal revolution and sometimes by invasion and conquest by neighboring nomadic tribes, mostly from Mongolia and Manchuria, that repeatedly replaced one ruling class with another. But through all these political changes and turmoil, the essential core of Chinese civilization remained intact. Even the creative center of all that China stood for was shifted from time to time, with the capital moving from one city to another, and during one period when the country was divided into a northern and southern kingdom, each had its own capital. Yet through all these vicissitudes, Chinese civilization did not perish, but appeared to emerge from each episode in some way refreshed and reinvigorated. And today we see China, after an interlude of prostration, exhibiting once more a strength and vitality that belie the notion that old civilizations die or else, like old soldiers, just fade away. It is true that the China of today is being profoundly affected by a foreign political system and an alien civilization. But this is nothing new in her history. It is too early to know whether she will absorb and modify them to her own basic civilization, as she has with other influences in the past, or will become an eastern extension of the Russian way of life. The important thing, however, is that the Chinese identity has survived; it has not been conquered or destroyed, and it still has the opportunity of continuing as a Chinese civilization.

China, in a sense, has been unique among the centers of civilization, which may partly account for the continuity and the remarkable strength of her traditions. China has developed in relative isolation, apparently stimulated from time to time by foreign ideas but too far removed from other centers of contemporary civilization to be physically threatened by them. India, which was the source of the Buddhist influence that carried in its train a series of ideas highly stimulating to Chinese civilization, was too far distant from China ever to molest or interfere with her development. The invasions she did suffer were from barbarous tribesmen who were merely seeking loot or, if remaining to conquer, possessed nothing in the way of a civilization to replace the one they had subdued. Unable to destroy Chinese civilization, they adopted it or were engulfed by it. Moreover, the large population that China embraced made her civilization difficult to stamp out deliberately, particularly in a country that was vast enough to provide room for retreat and rebound.

Something of the same history applies to India. If we date the beginning of her civilized life from the time when Harappa and Mohenjo-Daro flourished, she can claim an existence of at least forty-five hundred years. Closer to the centers of high civilization in the Near East and geographically more accessible to them, India was affected more profoundly by influences spreading from there than was China. And the incursions that India suffered during this time and later were perhaps more disruptive of the kind of unbroken continuity characteristic of China. Despite this, an Indian tradition was maintained through all these centuries. Even the domination of the British for several hundred years, although it introduced some aspects of Western civilization, was unable to alter the fundamental patterns of the civilization of India. As in China, the center of creative activity moved about in this subcontinent, and although these various geographical shifts are associated with special characteristics derived from local influences, the heritage of India was passed on, modified but unbroken.

Both China and India, at various periods in their histories, went through expansive phases during which they established satellite civilizations, some of which have disappeared while others have continued. These offshoots of the parental civilizations showed initially strong imitative tendencies, with an increasingly indigenous flavor as time permitted the fusion of the local culture with foreign influences. In this way the originally small foci of civilizations in the Yellow River Delta of China and the Indus Valley of India spread to Korea, Japan, Indochina (including the Cham and Cambodia), Tibet, Thailand, Assam, Java, and so on. It is, however, important to note that this diffusion and spread of Chinese and Indian civilizations did not end in their extinction in the original seats of development.

In the West, civilization appears from the available archaeological evidence to be older than in the East. Although an initial date for something so nebulous as the appearance of civilization is difficult to set to everyone's satisfaction, I think most authorities would agree that it is at least five thousand years old in Egypt and possibly still older in the Mesopotamian region. Egypt, for somewhat different reasons from those accounting for the preservation of the continuity of Chinese and Indian traditions, also, however, maintained its integrity for a comparable length of time—about three thousand years, if we date the end of its tradition with the Ptolemies and the Roman Conquest. By the time the Arabs replaced the Romans, the Egyptian civilization had been long dead and survived, then as now, only as an echo of a glorious past. Within this time, however, the spirit of Egypt was remarkably well defined. Perhaps more than anywhere else, the patterns of its expression were conservative, steady and undeviating. Although one can detect stylistic changes and variations in creative vigor throughout this span of time, the distinctive features of the civilization show relatively little alteration.

The peculiar geography of Egypt had perhaps something to do with this interesting pattern. The enormous fertility of the Nile Valley, renewing itself from year to year by the silts brought down from the distant hills of Abyssinia, provided an inexhaustible source of wealth in terms of produce. Thus the economy had an extraordinarily firm and continuous support. The exhaustion of resources and the fluctuation of climate that could, and apparently did, stimulate expansive movements elsewhere, were not significant here. The Nile Valley, moreover, is flanked by wide areas of extreme aridity that were like dry moats protecting the

country from invading enemies and discouraging
the growth of competing civilizations on its immediate flanks. Thus Egypt was protected for long
periods of time from the inroads of ambitious
powers and, considering the level of her attainments, made but few sustained efforts to extend her
hegemony beyond the Nile or to set up branch civilizations deriving their inspiration directly from
her. Even the invasion of the Hittites was short-
lived and of slight significance in deflecting her
traditions from their appointed course. Egyptian
influences were mainly by cultural diffusion and
by trade. Later, as the entire eastern Mediterranean filled up with spreading centers of civilization, Egypt was affected by and, in turn, influenced
these thriving cities and empires.

In the Near East, however, the situation was
quite different. Although civilization in its full
sense was first precipitated here in the Tigris-Euphrates area, it was not to remain confined to this
region but spread throughout most of the Near
East. This was, compared with Egypt, an area of
distinct turbulence and competition between states
and empires. Repeatedly Mesopotamia, and later
all of the Near East, was the scene of invasion
by surrounding tribes or of revolt by conquered

groups, each overthrowing its predecessor or neighbors and establishing new cities, new kingdoms and new empires. We know of a large number of distinct dynasties, different linguistic, cultural and ethnic groups competing with and overthrowing one another. To name only some of them may give an idea of the complexity of the history of the region. The earliest were the Sumerians, who were later united with the Akkadians from the north. We next hear of Babylonians, Mitannians, Kassites, Assyrians, Hittites, the Medes and Persians, the Chaldeans, Parthians, Sassanians, Arabs and Turks, not to mention the city states that enjoyed periods of independent autonomy of varying lengths.

Some justification for the general tendency to regard these ancient dynasties and empires as distinct civilizations may be drawn from the fact that many of them arose from diverse cultural origins, from different linguistic and ethnic groups, and developed new syntheses and special features of their own. This very diversity, moreover, has reinforced the organic concept of history, for in distinguishing the various actors and in attempting to trace the complex interrelationships of the tangled skein of their histories, their differences have been emphasized. There consequently emerges the ster-

eotype that assigns the Sumerians, the Hittites and
the Persians, for example, to distinct and independent civilizations as if they had no relationship to
each other. But this is a representation of Near
Eastern history that no archaeologist familiar with
the evidence would necessarily endorse. Despite the
high mortality rate of kingdom and empire and the
diversity of people, the civilization of one served
as the basis for its successor, and even contemporary
empires shared far more than is commonly realized.

The situation in Asia Minor was not unlike
what has occurred in Europe. Just as Rome provided the foundations of civilized life, on which
the various nations of Western Europe constructed
their versions of Western civilization, so the nu-
merous kingdoms and empires of the Near East
built upon the tradition of civilization established
first in Mesopotamia by the Sumerians and Akkadians. Moreover the diversity of ethnic, linguistic and local culture that has created in Europe
extreme variety within a single tradition and a
highly competitive array of states is paralleled by
what happened long ago in the Near East. Although the nationalistic and competitive nature of
the European system emphasizes differences by re-
ferring to French civilization, or British civiliza-

tion, or German *Kultur*, the fact remains that they are fundamentally members of one civilization with a common heritage from Rome, and they have borrowed extensively from one another.

Two truisms in anthropology are nowhere better illustrated than in the Near East. One of these is that centers of civilization tend to be expansive and to diffuse their ideas to adjacent areas. We have seen this in the case of China and India and can observe it in our own day. The other is that new centers of civilization, with few exceptions, do not appear suddenly complete—like Pallas Athene springing forth fully armed from the brow of Jupiter. Even though these new foci of civilization may eventually achieve greater heights, or merely different configurations, they begin on the foundations of what they have inherited from the civilizations before them.

The civilization that began its career in the cities of the Tigris-Euphrates valley thus expanded its influence, by diffusion and by the establishment of new centers of activity, until, reaching the Mediterranean littoral, it included Asia Minor in its orbit. Along the shores of Asia Minor the Ionian cities arose from the accumulated humus of centuries of civilization. In Crete a related civilization, partly influenced by Egypt, also took root in the same tradition. From these sources a stream of civilization, locally known as Mycenaean, reached Greece.

Far more than our conventional histories indicate, Greece borrowed heavily from her civilized neighbors in the beginning, but what she began by copying, her genius transformed into achievements that became distinctly her own. How much Rome owed to Asia Minor through the Etruscans we are only now beginning to appreciate. Her debt to Greece, however, has long been known. Thus expansion and rebuilding on older models carried the civilization of Mesopotamia farther and farther westward. Rome herself, in turn, eventually became a center of influence. But it is significant that Rome meant much more for the barbarous areas to the north and west than she did for the east, where older centers of civilization had continued along paths of their own development. Rome, as a fountainhead of culture for Europe, was actually reinforcing one stream of influence from Asia Minor and Greece, that had for millennia been entering the continent via the Danube and contributing to the growth of culture there, and another that is believed to have reached Europe via North Africa.

With the destruction of the Roman Empire, the influences established by Rome in France, Spain, Britain and other countries of Europe now ceased. But in the centuries that followed, her civilization, now fused with local traditions, provided the centers of new civilized life in Modern Europe. And early in their development these centers absorbed ideas from ancient sources in Asia Minor, from the Byzantine Empire and from the Arabs, all of them inheritors of a complex of civilization that evolved long ago in the Near East.

The view that Western civilization stems only from Greece and Rome is thus no longer tenable. Its roots extend widely and deeply into the Mesopotamian past, and its life has been continuous from these beginnings. Europe forms, consequently, with Asia Minor and North Africa, a geographic orbit comparable to China and India, within which a tradition of civilization has migrated but has also continued from its inception. Unlike the Chinese, Indian and Egyptian continuities, this one stemming from the Near East has had a more varied course and has produced in its long history a far greater richness of cultural expression and, in our time, has overleaped its ancient boundaries to seat itself in widely separated regions of the earth.

It is worth noting that in Toynbee's list of distinct civilizations, apart from those he calls "abortive" and those whose development occurred in the New World, there are fifteen that can be assigned to the Old World. Egypt has one, India two, China one, and eleven fall in the geographic orbit of Europe and the Near East. This excessive number for one region seems odd until one realizes that virtually all of them are essentially local, or national, expressions that are either related to, or are derived from, one another. This extreme proliferation strikes me as a significant reflection of the vitality of the civilization of this area. And it also reveals the way our historical perspectives tend to distort our concept of the growth of civilizations by presenting it in nationalized fragments.

Civilization, as we have seen, does not die like an organism. Actually, of the four principal traditions in the Old World, three have maintained an existence from their beginnings to the present time, modified by time and circumstances, but continuous. Since there is good reason to believe that all the civilizations of the Old World have a common source and have borrowed from one another, they can in one sense be regarded as diverse manifestations of a multifarious but single tradition of extraordinary vitality and persistence. From its first appearance, then, as a distinct way of life, civilization has never ceased to exist in one seat or another. The way a civilization may survive, even though it has apparently received a mortal blow, is illustrated by Rome. When the Roman Empire fell in the West, its civilization did not completely collapse with its political structure. It continued in the Eastern Empire. And by the time European centers had arisen, it was still a living reservoir from which they could draw, not to mention its indirect influences via the Arabs who transmitted so much precious freight to the same consumers in the West.

PATTERNS IN CIVILIZATION

If civilization itself does not go through organic cycles and eventually perish, it is still a constantly changing phenomenon that leaves in its wake outgrown institutions, abandoned styles, obsolete technologies and sterile ideas. No civilization, even if continuous in one place, as in Egypt and China, has remained unchanging with time. Let us look briefly at some more familiar to us than those whose past we know only inadequately from archaeological remains.

Although civilized life in England began in Roman times, the England we know today dates from William the Conqueror. From 1066 to the present is roughly nine hundred years. During this long period of time, England has suffered no invasions of foreign populations, no conquests by competing kingdoms, no overturns of the native civilization. Yet changes of the most profound kind have occurred through processes that affect it, as well as every other culture and civilization. And today we are witnessing still another transformation that would make contemporary Britain seem incomprehensible to an eighteenth-century Englishman, as his England might seem strange to a contemporary Briton. If these two periods, separated by two centuries, are divided as they are by so many alterations, both of them are equally modified from the times of Elizabeth or of Chaucer. Not only has a whole way of life been transformed, but political and social institutions, economy, architecture, art,

music, literature and science have also undergone
revolutionary changes.

What is true for Britain is, in varying degrees,
true for France, Italy, Spain and other European
countries. All of them reveal patterns of change
and modifications of such a profound nature that
we perforce differentiate them by such terms as
Gothic Age, the Renaissance and the Modern Age.
It is easy to trace the steps that have led from one
to the other and thus establish their continuity,
because the historical documentation is fresh and
abundant. I venture to suggest that the gulf between ourselves and the Romans is no greater, and
may be less, than that between ourselves and medieval Europeans, to whom we stand much closer
and from whom we have actually inherited our
traditions in an unbroken succession. The medieval world, through the changes that have transformed it step by step into the modern world, has
become extinct and, as far as we are concerned, a
different civilization from our own.

In these instances drawn from recent European history we can see civilization gradually going
through transformations of the most profound order, constantly changing within various European

national traditions. The integrity of the process does not, however, depend altogether on national or political continuity, as it may sometimes seem to do. When the city states of Greece were conquered and eventually absorbed into the Roman Empire, Greek civilization did not thereby end. Enough vitality remained in it to influence Rome profoundly for a long time and to continue in the eastern Mediterranean for many centuries thereafter, being gradually transformed as the matrix which supported it changed its character.

Change, then, is an integral part of civilization, just as it is in the simpler organizations of human behavior that we distinguish as primitive cultures. It is an error to assume that change is necessarily linked to a cycle of growth and death, comparable to the life of an organism, or that it necessarily implies progress. Progress, in the sense of an increasing ability to use and understand the environment and thus to produce an increasing complexity and variety in our behavior, has in a general way characterized the course of civilization as far as we can trace it. Many of the trends and modifications of the past do not follow this line, but represent adaptations, adjustments or the fulfillment of patterns that have nothing to do with progress as such, any more than mere movement necessarily means direction.

Although volumes have been written about the dynamics of change in civilization, it is a subject we cannot yet claim to understand in all its fullness. How complex and baffling it is, is nowhere better illustrated than in Professor Sorokin's monumental studies of some of its ramifications. If, therefore, I concern myself here with a very limited aspect of the total problem, it is because I could not hope to do justice to it in the conclusion of a brief essay, but more important, because I have a more restricted aim in mind. I should like merely to draw from certain features of the process some generalizations that seem to me throw light on the nature and growth of our own system of Western civilization.

In commenting on civilization in the United States, scholars and observers have generally been somewhat confused about the nature of its development. Europeans in particular have been ambivalent in their attitude. Professing to be interested above all in what is peculiar and native to us, they are at the same time critical of departures from their norms. If our artists and writers do conform to their patterns, they are apt to be dismissed as imitative. The fact that we have no dramatic poets like Shakespeare, no classic or romantic composers like Mozart or Beethoven, no painters in the Renaissance tradition, is somehow held against us as a failure in creative activity and as evidence of an inability to produce first-rate products of civilization.

This attitude might not be taken too much to heart if it did not also affect our own critics and, to some extent, our own artists, writers and composers. Americans, certainly in the past, have suffered in this regard from something like a split personality. If they did what all creative artists and writers must do: work from a tradition, they found themselves following the only tradition they had, namely, Europe's. Generally this produced, as imitation is likely to do, simply pale copies of European models. Emerson, for example, drew from Carlyle and German transcendentalism. Longfellow frequently tried to recreate outmoded European patterns in his epics and balladry. The value of both of them has been diminished by this derivation. Where a Thoreau, on the contrary, worked from native materials, he was ignored and left unread. I do not mean to imply that Thoreau, or even Whitman, failed to receive public recognition merely because he was not working along European lines. The originality of these men might just as well have prevented contemporary recognition in another culture; but the American public, conditioned by European models, found American copies of them more congenial and easier to absorb. Not until a native tradition had become established could new works of a distinctly American origin and style be expected to win a ready acceptance.

What we fail to realize in appraising American civilization is that when we try to transplant a tradition from one region to another a certain process is involved, and critics unaware of the effect of such a transfer can be both captious and unjust. To begin with, the flower of civilized life is a tender bloom and cannot be expected to survive such an experience undamaged. In the case of the United States, the transplantation was to a wilderness, and civilization, to flourish at all, demands levels of economic and social development that simply did not exist in America. That America produced no creative works worth mentioning in the first two centuries of her existence is not in the least surprising. The remarkable thing was not how little was produced in the Colonies but how much intellectual activity of a superior, if arid, kind did manage to thrive in New England, where little if anything might have been looked for, since life was on a relatively primitive plane.

Although even from the earliest days there were some cultivated men scattered throughout the Colonies and learning was tenderly nourished in a few places, the basis for a genuine civilization did not take form until cities and towns began to spring up along the Atlantic seaboard during the seventeenth and eighteenth centuries. They were at first frail supports for the development of a true civilization, but as their prosperity increased, they became significant importers of ideas from Europe. In these growing urban centers, limners and painters could find enough commissions to set up studios; books could find a market; companies of actors could gather audiences; and the colonists began to accumulate wealth with which to erect imposing buildings. Since there was nothing of this sort indigenous to America that the colonists could use, they borrowed wholeheartedly and avidly from Europe. That is the way civilization spreads and it is virtually the only way. Imitation is the first step in establishing a new center of civilization. This is the stage when pride centers not on being different but on being as like the mother country as possible. What was fashionable in London or Paris became automatically the inexorable standard for the Colonies. Athens and Paris and London, in their time, went through a similar imitative phase in their initial development as centers of civilization.

When the first sustained burst of creative activity occurred in the early nineteenth century, our native writers and artists copied European models, quite frankly and without shame. The idea that they somehow ought to be creating in a native American idiom probably did not occur to them as an obligation. They quite happily produced Columbiads after English Dunciads. Our Wests and Copleys went to school in England and remained minor British artists.

It was characteristic that as America borrowed from Europe, she took off from precisely the point that European patterns had then reached. The borrowing process seems always to involve a branching off at the latest phase of a pattern of development. In other words, our poets were copying not Shakespeare but Pope; our composers, when we began to produce them later in the nineteenth century, were too late to imitate Mozart, and instead found Brahms and Tschaikowski more appropriate models. Thus our beginnings did not retrace the initial phases of European patterns. When Longfellow tried to recreate in *Hiawatha* the epic form long abandoned in European literature, he was being archaistic, artificial and unconvincing. *Hiawatha* was never a genuine production. Nothing is so dead as an outmoded style—in hats or in literature.

It would be presumptuous to say that the reason we have never produced a Shakespeare or a Marlowe is because we arrived too late, but it is certainly the reason none of our poets tried to be like them. And it is the reason we have never genuinely created in this country certain types of literature, music or art that have existed in Europe. There are some apparent exceptions to this rule, the most notable being our attempts to recreate Gothic, Romanesque, Greek and other types of European buildings long after their heyday. But architecture, more than the other arts, tends to be eclectic and imitative of the past. And our reconstructions, after all, were not essentially different from what contemporary Europeans were also doing with the same architectural styles.

This conditioning of the development of a new civilization depends upon the nature of patterns of change. Kroeber has called attention to the tendency of change to proceed in a definite pattern until its potentialities have been exhausted. Consequently, one observes that creators in a developed or late stage of the pattern tend to avoid styles and forms characteristic of an earlier phase. So our painters of today would scarcely attempt to paint like Rubens or Watteau. They are committed, in a sense, to a fulfillment of a pattern of change. For this reason the character of the new civilization is deeply affected at first by the stage of development of the present civilization from which it stems.

But although imitation necessarily marked the apprenticeship of America, the modification of the European institutions and culture the colonists brought here began almost at once. This, as a general rule, is what happens when cultures are carried to a new environment. If the transplantation is followed by isolation from the mother country, one might expect the adaptation to express itself rather more rapidly than if contacts are continued. In the United States these contacts were maintained with increasing, rather than diminishing, frequency and variety, and they served to keep our civilization in a colonial frame of mind even after political independence had been achieved. But as adaptation continues and the independent lines of

change in language, institutions, values, behavior
and in various other ways deepen, they inevitably
influence the creative productions of the country.
Out of this comes a new synthesis and a recogniz-
ably different phase of the parent civilization. It is
difficult to predict when this will happen, since it
depends on so many intangibles. In many ways the
evidence that we have entered such a stage is becoming clear. Whether it will lead to a major manifestation, or remain simply a local aspect of Western civilization, is beyond prediction.

It would be unrealistic to anticipate a completely
new kind of civilization in the United States without counterpart elsewhere. We are, after all, the
inheritors of Western civilization just as much as
are the Europeans, and our common roots will continue to provide a family relationship. The various
European countries, for all their differences, have
much in common. Moreover, it is in the nature of
the contact between civilizations that, when they
are on a basis of approximate equality, they borrow
from one another. This diffusion tends to redis-
tribute new ideas and break down extreme differentiation. The road of communication between
Europe and America has widened from a single
track headed this way into a two-lane highway with

traffic moving in both directions. The United States has emerged from its purely imitative stage, and has become a contributor to Western civilization.

Date Due			
Feb. 9			
Feb. 13			
Feb 27			
apr. 16			
4/30			
			13